101 Ways to Score Higher on Your LSAT

What You Need to Know About the Law School Admission Test Explained Simply

By Linda C. Ashar

101 Ways to Score Higher on Your LSAT: What You Need to Know About the Law Schoolt Admission Test Explained Simply

ISBN-13: 978-1-60138-253-5   ISBN-10: 1-60138-253-7

Library of Congress Cataloging-in-Publication Data

Ashar, Linda C., 1947-
   101 ways to score higher on your LSAT : what you need to know about the law school admission test explained simply / by Linda C. Ashar.
      p. cm.
   Includes bibliographical references and index.
   ISBN-13: 978-1-60138-253-5 (alk. paper)
   ISBN-10: 1-60138-253-7 (alk. paper)
   1. Law schools--United States--Entrance examinations. 2. Law School Admission Test. I. Title. II. Title: One hundred one ways to score higher on your LSAT. III. Title: One hundred and one ways to score higher on your LSAT.

KF285.Z9A15 2008
340.076--dc22
                            20080356519

INTERIOR LAYOUT DESIGN: Vickie Taylor • vtaylor@atlantic-pub.com
PROJECT MANAGER: Angela Adams • aadams@atlantic-pub.com

Printed in the United States

Printed on Recycled Paper

Dedication

To my husband Michael,
the best lawyer I know.

We recently lost our beloved pet "Bear," who was not only our best and dearest friend but also the "Vice President of Sunshine" here at Atlantic Publishing. He did not receive a salary but worked tirelessly 24 hours a day to please his parents. Bear was a rescue dog that turned around and showered myself, my wife Sherri, his grandparents Jean, Bob and Nancy and every person and animal he met (maybe not rabbits) with friendship and love. He made a lot of people smile every day.

We wanted you to know that a portion of the profits of this book will be donated to The Humane Society of the United States.

–Douglas & Sherri Brown

THE HUMANE SOCIETY OF THE UNITED STATES©

The human-animal bond is as old as human history. We cherish our animal companions for their unconditional affection and acceptance. We feel a thrill when we glimpse wild creatures in their natural habitat or in our own backyard.

Unfortunately, the human-animal bond has at times been weakened. Humans have exploited some animal species to the point of extinction.

The Humane Society of the United States makes a difference in the lives of animals here at home and worldwide. The HSUS is dedicated to creating a world where our relationship with animals is guided by compassion. We seek a truly humane society in which animals are respected for their intrinsic value, and where the human-animal bond is strong.

Want to help animals? We have plenty of suggestions. Adopt a pet from a local shelter, join The Humane Society and be a part of our work to help companion animals and wildlife. You will be funding our educational, legislative, investigative and outreach projects in the U.S. and across the globe.

Or perhaps you'd like to make a memorial donation in honor of a pet, friend or relative? You can through our Kindred Spirits program. And if you'd like to contribute in a more structured way, our Planned Giving Office has suggestions about estate planning, annuities, and even gifts of stock that avoid capital gains taxes.

Maybe you have land that you would like to preserve as a lasting habitat for wildlife. Our Wildlife Land Trust can help you. Perhaps the land you want to share is a backyard—that's enough. Our Urban Wildlife Sanctuary Program will show you how to create a habitat for your wild neighbors.

So you see, it's easy to help animals. And The HSUS is here to help.

The Humane Society of the United States
2100 L Street NW
Washington, DC 20037
202-452-1100
www.hsus.org

Courtroom Testimony: Attorney Examining Witness

ATTORNEY: Doctor, before you performed the autopsy, did you check for a pulse?

WITNESS: No.

ATTORNEY: Did you check for blood pressure?

WITNESS: No.

ATTORNEY: Did you check for breathing?

WITNESS: No

ATTORNEY: So, then it is possible that the patient was alive when you began the autopsy?

WITNESS: No.

ATTORNEY: How can you be so sure, Doctor?

WITNESS: Because his brain was sitting in a jar on my desk.

ATTORNEY: But could the patient have still been alive, nevertheless?

WITNESS: Yes, it is possible that he could have been alive and practicing law.

From courtroom public records compiled in: Disorder in the Court: Great Fractured Moments in Courtroom History, by Charles M. Sevilla and Lee Lorenz, 1999, excerpt as quoted at www.cruiserjim. com/AmericanCourts.htm, March 1, 2008.

Table of Contents

Chapter 2: Assessing Your LSAT Acumen 75

Chapter 3: Designing a Holistic Preparation Plan 81

Chapter 6: The Writing Sample 231

Chapter 7: Test Day 239

Chapter 8: On a Lighter Note............245

Chapter 9: Case Studies 247

Conclusion 269

1

Introduction to Law School & the LSAT

Described by *The Washington Times* as, "one of the most grueling admissions tests in the world," the Law School Admission Test — the notorious LSAT — is one of the rites of passage, a threshold, into the legal profession. It is the first of many tests to challenge — and perhaps discourage - would-be lawyers.

All kinds of words have been used to describe the LSAT, many of them censorable. Regardless of what anyone says about it, such as unbelievable, unfair, incomprehensible, nightmarish, crazy, senseless, sadistic, and worse, the LSAT remains a required component of the admissions process for all American Bar Association (ABA) accredited law schools, most non-ABA accredited law schools, and most Canadian law schools.

The LSAT is devised, studied, administered, and scored by an independent agency, the Law School Admissions Council (LSAC). The LSAT score, ranging from the highest possible at 180 to a rock bottom 120, is a core criterion assessed by law schools for selecting their new crop of first-year students. While it is ostensibly only one of several considerations that law school admissions officers consider when making their final selection from the pool of law school applicants, no one can seriously dispute that the LSAT score continues to be one of the most important, even the most important, consideration. Metaphorically speaking, you must approach it with your brain in your head, not in a jar on your desk.

1. Understand the Law School Application Process

If there is one overriding rule about the law school application process and preparing for the LSAT as part of it, that rule is do not procrastinate. If you do you will plunge yourself into a spiraling time crunch that will negatively impact your ability to timely schedule, and achieve a high score on the LSAT. The prevailing wisdom is to start your application process in January of the year before you expect to matriculate which is approximately 18 months ahead of time. The latest you might be able to wait and still slip in is about nine months in advance, but in most cases, that would be truly pushing the envelope. As illustrated in one of the Case Studies in Chapter 9, Kathy Daly, now a successful New York lawyer, is living proof that the latter can be done.

The Princeton Review, which publishes a comprehensive LSAT prep book, *Cracking the LSAT*, offers its one of several online services to assist students in matching schools to their needs and expectations. This service invites schools to coordinate their recruitment efforts with *The Princeton Review's* comprehensive resources.

Although most are procedurally similar, each law school has its own application process. Pay attention to deadlines; answer all the questions without trying to second guess why they are asked; assemble the materials required; order transcripts; and register for the LSAT.

For most law schools, one of the important pieces in the application process is the personal statement. This is considered a necessary component of the application because it reflects the applicant's ability to express himself or herself in writing, and explains why he or she is a good candidate for law school. Intended to put their best foot forward and catch the eye of the admissions committee, many students use professional services, personal editors, and even ghostwriters to assist them. It is no secret that these writing services are found easily on the Internet. Some law schools use an LSAT writing sample to compare applicants writing styles with their personal statements. The personal statement thus is balanced by the greatest equalizer in the law school application process — the notorious LSAT.

2. Understand How the LSAT is Scored

LSAT Scoring

The lowest possible score on the LSAT is 120, the highest is 180, and the national median is 151. These numbers represent a scaled score based on the number of correct answers. Because the tests vary in difficulty, the scaled score for each test is further classified by a percentile according to how all the test takers performed on that edition of the test. The percentile score is considered the best indicator of performance. To be in the 50th percentile range, you must answer about 56 out of 101 questions correctly, or have a score of 151. A total raw score of 75 will yield a scaled score of 163 to 165, which generally places a student into the 90th percentile. This is a jump of 40 percent while answering only 19 additional questions correctly.

Most people assume that a perfect 180 on the LSAT means not missing any questions, but in some cases, you can miss up to five questions, and still have a scaled score of 180. Answering just a few more questions can significantly effect your percentile ranking.

This is the value of preparing for the LSAT. Preparation makes the difference between a so-so score and an excellent score; you have studied, are at ease with your testing ability and have become familiar with the LSAT process. It is the difference between spending half a day with a dragon rather than a tame pussycat.

3. Know the LSAT Score You Need to Hit for Your Chosen Schools

The minimum LSAT score you need to achieve will depend on the law school you hope to enter. The highest ranked schools will be the most selective. Lower ranked schools may have lower requirements for admission in terms of the LSAT score, but a law school's overall lower ranking by the published list makers does not mean that the school produces bad lawyers. The reality of the legal marketplace is this; the more prestigious the law school, the more opportunities its graduates have in getting a first job offer. There are many good law schools to choose from in both the United States and Canada. Most experts agree that higher LSAT scores bring more job choices and fewer worries.

Whether your choice of law schools is controlled by location, tuition costs, or career goals, you should do your homework before applying. Educate yourself about each potential school's admissions policy, standards, and procedures. In particular, find out where your LSAT score needs to fall to put you in the top field of applicants. "The higher the better" is a nice broad statement, but it does not define the ballpark of realistic and specific requirements for each school.

4. Know What Your Law School Choices Require

There are various sources that rank law schools by the range of LSAT scores of the students they have selected for admission. Also, some law schools publish this information on their Web sites or in their application materials.

For a global survey of the law school marketplace, there are several sources that publish lists ranking law schools according to level of prestige. What makes a school prestigious is the sum of a variety of factors ranging from historical clout of social and business elitism, to the median calculation of student scores, GPAs, and versatility of talent the schools attract, and how its graduates compete in the real world after graduation.

You may consult these lists to see where your potential choices fall, and also obtain guidance for where you wish to apply. Most of the list-makers ranking law schools state that they use a composite of various factors to determine their choice of top schools. Here are three list-makers who employ such a composite of factors.

The Consus Group (TCG) is a company founded by California lawyers and management consultants. They use a composite scoring formula for ranking law schools including a law school's historic ranking by other sources, certain selectivity factors (with the LSAT weighted at 35 percent), starting salaries of the school's graduates, the school's success in placing its graduates, and the percentage of students tapped for admission who actually attend the school.

www.LawSchool100.com (LS100) is an online list published by LawTV, Inc. that purports to select its top "A" list of first-tier, top 100 law schools in the United States "based on qualitative, rather than quantitative, criteria." Also, LS100 lists a "B" list of second-tier law schools.

U.S. News & World Report (NWR), a well-known and long-established current events news service, lists its choice of top 100 law schools according to a survey it sends out to law schools. Similar to TCG, NWR's ranking criteria include "selectivity" factors, part of which is a median of the LSAT scores of students admitted by each of the law schools surveyed.

The following table shows a comparative selection from these three groups' rankings of their respective picks for the top 100 law schools for 2008.

TCG	LS100	NWR
1st Yale Law School	1st Harvard Law School	1st Yale Law School
2nd Harvard Law School	2nd Stanford U. Law	2nd Harvard Law School
3rd Stanford U. Law	2nd Yale Law School (tied with Stanford)	3rd Stanford U. Law
4th Columbia Law School	4th NYU Law School	4th NYU Law School

TCG	LS100	NWR
5th NYU Law School	4th Columbia Law School (tied with NYU)	5th Columbia Law School
	4th U. of Chicago Law (tied with NYU)	
...	...	...
82nd Richardson Law (Hawaii)	85th Syracuse U. Law	91st Richardson Law (Hawaii)
100th Syracuse U. Law	97th Richardson Law (Hawaii) One of 12 tied for 97th Place None below 97th due to ties	100th U. of the Pacific*
* Syracuse University Law is not listed in NWR's top 100 ranking law schools		

A fourth list-maker, **www.top-law-schools.com**, ranks the same top-five law schools as above and in exactly the same order as NWR's list for 2008.

Although there is some variance where individual schools place on these lists, there is significant agreement among all these sources as to which schools rank in the top 100, and where those schools fall on the list — especially the top five. Even though each list-maker considers its own formula of factors for ranking, all include the applicants' LSAT scores and Grade Point Averages (GPA). Without question, in all such rankings, the law schools' LSAT score acceptance range emerges as an essential and constant component in each list-maker's calculations. Higher LSAT scores consistently correspond to higher-ranked law schools. This obvious importance of the LSAT, notwithstanding, top-ranked Yale Law School advises that the LSAT is only one of many factors in its evaluation of applicants. Yale states on its Web site, "we take all the information available to us into account," and "no one factor . . . will be dispositive."

One would expect Yale, or any school, to utilize a multi-dimensional evaluation of applicants, but if the LSAT is not the "single" determiner for highly-ranked Yale, it clearly correlates with the other factors considered important, such as a student's high GPA. Another publisher of law school rankings is Internet Legal Research Group (ILRG), which provides its 2008 list of 184 law schools ranked simply according to highest and lowest LSAT scores of students admitted, and the corresponding GPA ranges. Yale Law School is number one on ILRG's list for 2008. Yale's highest reported LSAT score was 176 and the lowest score was 170, with a corresponding GPA range of 3.97 to 3.83. Virtually the same data for Yale is reported on the NWR list. Yale itself reports the LSAT range for its graduate class of 2010 (2006 matriculation) as 177 to 170. Yale further reports that, ultimately, it tapped only 226 applicants for admission out of 3,313 hopefuls for that class, of which 189 actually matriculated. To put these numbers in perspective — Yale Law accepted only 6.82 percent of its pool of applicants that year; 5.7 percent matriculated.

Yale Law would have considered, of course, many factors along the way in making its final cut to 226 applicants. But certainly LSAT performance is the undeniably significant tool they used to whittle 3,313 applicants down to a manageable number. Yale's accepted LSAT score range is consistently 170 or higher. While a high LSAT score alone may not be the dispositive final factor in every individual acceptance, an applicant is not likely to be in the running without it. Surely, he or she will need the score to make at least the first cut. Also notable is the tight cluster of the Yale's admittees' incredibly high LSAT scores, spanning a mere six points, with the bottom score of 170 being only ten points off the LSAT "perfect" 180. For the other four top-five schools, ILRG reported similar LSAT acceptance ranges for 2008: Harvard,

175-169; Columbia, 174-169; Stanford, 172-169; NYU, 172-168. There is so little disparity in the LSAT scores of the applicants accepted by the top-five law schools, it is easy to generalize where an applicant's LSAT score needs to be; for consideration by a top-ranked school, and presumably acceptable for any school, the safest minimum score for the top schools is 170.

Obviously, 170 is not the required minimum number for all schools. As a comparison to the top-five law schools on these lists, the lowest reported data on ILRG's 2008 list is Southern University Law School at 184th. Southern U. reports an LSAT score range of 149 -144, with a corresponding GPA range of 3.42 to 2.6. Southern University Law School does not appear on TCG, LS100 or NWR's top 100 lists, but LS100 does include Southern U. on its "B" list as a recognized second-tier law school.

Although the Canadian law schools seem to resist the allure of ranking, the following have been listed as the top-five of several fine Canadian law schools by **www.top-law-schools.com.**

1. University of Toronto

2. University of British Columbia

3. McGill University

4. York University

5. University of Ottawa

The admissions committee of the University of Toronto Law School advises on the school's Web site that it gives "greatest weight to an applicant's cumulative undergraduate academic record and

LSAT score." On the other hand, third-ranked McGill University states that the LSAT is "not mandatory" at all for admission, but that every applicant who has taken the LSAT is required to report his LSAT score and date of taking the test. Failure to do so will be an omission that disqualifies the applicant from consideration for admittance.

Perusal of these various top 100 lists and the top schools' accepted LSAT scores reveals the obvious direct correlation of high LSAT scores with highly ranked law schools: the higher the score, the better an applicant's chances of admission at any school. The overwhelming importance of the LSAT score cannot be plausibly denied. To make a case in point, Professor Pinello of the City University of New York proposes that an applicant with an undergraduate GPA of at least 3.5 and an LSAT score of 168 or higher has a 100 percent chance of being accepted by a law school like Fordham University — ranked 17th on ILRG's highest LSAT admission scores for 2008. Conversely, if that same applicant's LSAT score is 160 — a mere eight scaled points lower — Professor Pinello opines that the applicant's chance of acceptance drops to about 70 percent. With a score of 156, which is slightly above the national LSAT median, that applicant's chance of acceptance plummets to 15 percent.

Professor Pinello's assessment is not out of line with the reported law school LSAT score rankings for 2008. ILRG reports Fordham's 2008 high LSAT acceptance score at 167, and a low of 163, with a corresponding GPA range of 3.74 to 3.41. This evidently validates Professor Pinello's hypothetical 3.5 GPA applicant having assured acceptance with an LSAT score of 168; Fordham is ranked 25th by both LS100 and NWR, and 18th by TCG.

The reported law school statistics, crystallized by Professor Pinello's hypothetical assessment, indicate that a high LSAT score is customarily considered to be 168 or above — with the accent on above 168 for the top five schools. Although ILRG's and the other list rankings indicate that not all law schools require a high LSAT score for admission, most assuredly, a high LSAT score can do much to offset a less-than-stellar GPA, and perhaps other inglorious factors in the law school admissions world.

Without question, the higher the LSAT score, the more choices of law schools and scholarship opportunities a prospective law student is likely to have. Achieving just a few points higher on the LSAT significantly increases those choices and opportunities. Because of the LSAT's importance in the law school admission process, only the foolhardy approach the LSAT lightly or take it unprepared.

The significance of this test has fostered a burgeoning industry of LSAT how-to books, programs, courses, practice aids, tutors, mentors, study guides, and various combinations of these approaches. A survey of the major producers of LSAT preparatory materials suggests various methodologies to assist you in preparing for the LSAT and improving your LSAT score.

This book outlines ways for you to optimally prepare for and achieve a higher score on the LSAT, with emphasis on a holistic approach that will carry you not only through the LSAT with success, but also law school and beyond. These suggestions of various approaches and routines to improve LSAT performance are based on:

- Review of many print and online publications.

- The author's own experience and observations as a lawyer and educator.

- Interviews with law students and professionals in the LSAT prep world; some represented in the Case Studies included in this book.

- Law schools' admissions literature and Web sites.

- Internet commentaries and blogs.

- Some good old-fashioned common sense.

Which of these suggestions, or a specific combination of them, that will work best for you must ultimately be your decision. That decision should be based on an honest, careful assessment of your specific LSAT skills, learning style and strengths and weaknesses; and, not insignificantly, the constraints of life's demands on your schedule and your determination to master the LSAT's labyrinth of challenges. Like any puzzle, as the solution is revealed the challenge becomes increasingly easier. But without understanding the methodology underpinning the LSAT test questions, the solution alone will be meaningless.

There is no one specific formula to guarantee success; no magic sword to slay the dragon. The information provided in this book is not intended to present you comprehensive lists of LSAT practice test questions, but rather styles of questions and modes of thinking that are used in the LSAT, and ways to prepare yourself to take the test. Such comprehensive lists and practice questions along with tutors, mentors, and classroom courses are available in the plethora of resources on the LSAT market. Some of them are briefly quoted here where particularly helpful to the subject. In the Case Studies there are experts and LSAT survivors who have kindly contributed their valuable frontline advice. All of these sources have something to offer. You may find a combination of these resources works best for your ultimate preparatory approach.

Despite the many market sources that promise they can sell you a high LSAT score, though, the only trail to assured success is the one you blaze for yourself. Success in taking the LSAT requires a combination of:

- Innate intelligence

- Acquired skills

- Acquired knowledge

- Physical stamina

- Mental stamina

- Preparation

- Fortitude

- Organization

- Self-discipline

- and, more than a little bit of psychology

In the words of one LSAT veteran, pen-named "Cpetrako," writing on YouTube (**www.youtube.com**), "The LSAT is meant to break you. It's not the smartest people that get into LS [law school] but the toughest and most hard working. This is bible truth."

5. You Must Prepare Yourself

Getting into law school and staying there for the long haul is all about work and endurance. There is no magical short cut. Preparing yourself systematically and sensibly for the rigors of the LSAT will replace mystery and anxiety with knowledge and confidence. Your bywords are planning, preparation, and persistence. These same principles apply to success in law school as well. Seize the challenge and make the most of it.

6. Understand the LSAT's Purpose

Getting a high score on the LSAT begins with understanding what the test's creators at LSAC intend to accomplish. The LSAT is not just one test. It is a half-day series of tests allegedly designed to evaluate measurable lawyer skills, described by LSAC as "essential for success in law school." These skills include facility with language, organization and problem-solving skills, and the ability to function under pressure of a deadline. University of Toronto Law School's admissions policy validates the importance of these skills, and more, by summing up the qualities of the ideal law candidate on its Web site: "high intelligence, sound judgment, the capacity and motivation for demanding intellectual effort, the capacity and motivation to engage in sophisticated legal reasoning, and an understanding of and sensitivity to human interaction."

7. Critical Thinking Is at the Heart of LSAT Success

These desirable reasoning abilities are embodied in the concept of critical thinking. This is what the LSAT attempts to measure. In a broad sense, critical thinking involves the following types of mental exercises.

- Identifying and sorting through facts for selecting information relevant to analyzing and solving problems; often there will be facts included that you will not need to answer the questions; their role is to confuse, obfuscate and distract; if you are not reading closely or misunderstand the question, they will succeed.

- Organizing and systematically applying data for determining cause and effect, and reaching solutions to problems.

- Trying new or creative ways to resolve a problem; often referred to as "thinking outside the box," or "nonlinear thinking."

- Drawing inferences from evidence and information; inferential thinking is often intuitive; you may need to learn to recognize between evidence that is actually stated and the inferences you are automatically drawing from the evidence.

- Having the ability to draw analogies between different sets of information.

- Recognizing missing information.

- Recognizing faulty reasoning and missing assumptions; these are at the heart of flawed logic.

Every day a practicing lawyer is reading, writing, and speaking in courts, offices, conferences, and meeting rooms with clients, judges, witnesses and adversaries. The lawyer's work is not so much about knowing the law — although that is undeniably a piece of it. The lawyer studies and practices the law, and certainly is comfortable in finding the statute books and court decisions.

Theoretically at least, anyone can look up a specific law or read a court decision. Resources on the Internet have increased every person's ability to do just that. "Ignorance of the law is no excuse" is an axiom that applies to everybody after all — not just lawyers.

So what does a lawyer do?

8. Understand the Lawyer's Work

In its most profound incarnation, the law regulates human conduct and the inevitable disputes that arise between family members, neighbors, strangers, states, business conglomerates and nations. It is through its laws that a social group keeps the peace, defines its relationships, provides a structure for solving problems, and balances competing needs and demands of individual persons and groups. Consciously recognizing how this works will orient your thinking from the inside out in a way that will inherently improve your perception of the LSAT questions.

Law regulates every facet of society. Every transaction from borrowing a book from the public library to purchasing the Empire State Building, and every life event from cradle to grave — birth, marriage, work, housing, divorce, death, burial — invokes public and private legal requirements, procedures, rights and obligations.

The United States and Canada's legal systems operate on a system of statutes and regulations enacted by elected officials and governmentally appointed agencies. A system of law called the common law operates in tandem with these formally enacted laws and regulations.

The wording of statutes and regulations and the procedures under which they operate are subject to change by lawmakers, and further subject to interpretative rulings by the courts; the latter often called the "judicial gloss" on the statutes. Within the United States, these laws, regulations and procedures must be consonant with the structure of the United States Constitution and the constitutional framework of each of the 50 states; with special features in the state of Louisiana derived from French civil law. Lawyers themselves are instrumental in lawmaking, as they argue the meaning and intent of laws, reaching for new applications of the laws in the process of their advocacy for their clients.

Apart from legislative action, the common law has developed over centuries of judicial decisions as courts have grappled with balancing the rights and obligations brought before them in their communities. Courts decide the common law not by enactment but by analyzing the new cases pending before them, according to the dictates of legislation that may be applicable, and similar cases that have been decided by courts in the past. The prior cases provide a precedent, a basis, for a judge's consideration of a new case. The principle of a court's following precedent is called *stare decisis* — Latin for, "Let the decision stand."

Stare decisis is not a static concept. Although the courts look to prior decisions, not every case is the same; the lawyers and the courts struggle for a new decision that look to precedent, but in the act of applying it, the law is stretched and reshaped. The lawyers' role is to bring critical thinking to an understanding and knowledge of existing law, to advocate for their clients' rights and predicaments. Such reshaping happens cautiously and not easily, though when it does, it can be dramatically.

An example of *stare decisis* best explains the concept. In 1992 the United States Supreme Court considered a case called *Planned Parenthood of Southeast Pennsylvania v. Casey*. This case was about a Pennsylvania law on the socially controversial subject of abortion. Pennsylvania had enacted several legislative restrictions requiring a woman to give prior notice to various third parties, including the husband of a married woman, and 24-hour waiting periods before an abortion procedure could lawfully proceed. The constitutionality of the law's limitations on personal abortion decisions was challenged by Planned Parenthood on the basis of the 1973 United States Supreme Court case known as *Roe v. Wade*, the famous landmark case that made legal abortion possible in the United States as a matter of choice in at least the first trimester of a woman's pregnancy. *Roe v. Wade* was an example of one of those dramatic cases emerging from the common law as an example of Court–created law out of a Constitutional framework. In this case the Court recognized that abortion under certain circumstances could not be prohibited because under the United

States Constitution, a woman's right to choose was protected as a matter of right embodied in the right of privacy, a Constitutional liberty.

In ensuing years *Roe v. Wade* met with both much social criticism and much social support, and crystallized into pro-choice and pro-life supporters in the U.S. social environment. Various state laws responded to *Roe v. Wade* by placing restrictions on how abortions could be conducted; such as imposing waiting periods during which a woman would be advised of risks and options, and forcing her to take the time to change her mind. Also, parental notification of pregnant minors became an issue.

In *Planned Parenthood v. Casey*, Pennsylvania laws imposing a 24-hour delay in getting an abortion and new notification laws, including a married woman notifying her husband prior to an abortion, were challenged by Planned Parenthood as unreasonable barriers to the "liberty" underlying the right to an abortion recognized by the Court in *Roe v. Wade*. The eyes of both abortion rights and right-to-life advocates were on the Court in the Casey case because, as both society and the membership on the Court had changed since 1973, this new abortion rights case might have provided an opportunity for the Court to overrule the controversial *Roe v. Wade*. Here was a compelling case demonstrating what lawyers do.

Planned Parenthood relied upon the principle of *stare decisis*, on the basis of *Roe v. Wade*, making the following points in its argument to the Court.

1. The decision to terminate a pregnancy in the first trimester

is a fundamental privacy and liberty right as the Court has previously held in *Roe v. Wade*.

2. *Roe v. Wade*'s guarantee of safe, legal abortion has been of profound significance to the lives of American women.

3. To uphold the Pennsylvania law will result in overturning *Roe v. Wade*.

4. *Stare decisis* requires that *Roe v. Wade* be followed.

The State of Pennsylvania took two approaches to opposing this argument, first arguing that its law was constitutional and could be squared with *Roe v. Wade*. Even with this argument, Pennsylvania still invited the Court to overturn *Roe v. Wade*, stating, "the Court therefore need not, although it certainly may, use this case as a vehicle for re-examining Roe [v. Wade]." This is known as legally hedging your bet, or not putting all your eggs in the same basket. Pennsylvania essentially was saying, "in a minute, we are going to argue why the Court should overrule *Roe v. Wade* outright, but before we get there, our legal argument still works anyway." Then Pennsylvania proceeded to challenge the Court to overrule *Roe v. Wade* entirely and return all abortion rights decisions to each state to decide. Pennsylvania argued that *Roe v. Wade* "is a deeply flawed decision, and it may be that the time has come to reconsider it." Pennsylvania then continued to enumerate all the reasons why it believed the *Roe v. Wade* decision to be flawed.

Diametrically opposed positions were argued to the United States Supreme Court about how the law permitting abortion as defined in *Roe v. Wade* either should – or should not – be changed. Since the time of the controversial *Roe v. Wade* holding, American society had coalesced into pro-life and pro-choice camps; many people were watching the Court.

The Court, ultimately, took an interesting approach. It allowed some of Pennsylvania's requirements to stand, except for the spousal notification, which it overruled. It was significant that the Court declined to do what Pennsylvania truly was asking it to do, which was to overrule *Roe v. Wade*. Stating that "liberty finds no refuge in a jurisprudence of doubt," the Court explained its decision to leave *Roe v. Wade* in place on the basis of *stare decisis*, as follows:

"When this Court reexamines a prior holding, its judgment is customarily informed by a series of prudential and pragmatic considerations designed to test the consistency of overruling a prior decision with the ideal of the rule of law, and to gauge the respective costs of reaffirming and overruling a prior case. Thus, for example, we may ask whether the rule has proven to be intolerable simply in defying practical workability; whether the rule is subject to a kind of reliance that would lend a special hardship to the consequences of overruling and add inequity to the cost of repudiation; whether related principles of law have so far developed as to have left the old rule no more than a remnant of abandoned doctrine; or whether facts have so changed, or come to be seen so differently, as to have robbed the old rule of significant application or justification."

Note from the Court's words in this passage the great weight that is placed on the rule of law of the previous case. That weight is the heart of the meaning and purpose of *stare decisis*. If the case has been relied upon as the law of the land, it carries the day unless it has become no longer relevant or workable, in the

Court's words, a mere "remnant" of an "abandoned doctrine." Thus, in the *Planned Parenthood v. Casey* case, the lawyers arguing for upholding *Roe v. Wade* succeeded in persuading the Court to not depart from the principle of *stare decisis*. Yet, that principle does not always convince the Court.

As the Court's words in *Planned Parenthood v. Casey* suggest, there are times when *stare decisis* will not prevail in a case. Through artful persuasion presenting well-reasoned argument as to why a precedent is no longer valid — or perhaps never was for a given rule — a lawyer may prevail in changing the law despite the odds seemingly against him or her. A court can be persuaded a precedent does not apply, no longer applies, or was wrong in the first place. How can this happen? Another case in point illustrates the common law at work in counterpoint to *stare decisis*.

Historically, many laws in various states of the United States have banned certain types of consensual sexual conduct, both homosexual and heterosexual. One such state was Georgia, whose state law criminalized oral and anal sex acts whether engaged by homosexual or heterosexual partners, and defined them as the crime of sodomy, a serious felony which carried a potential jail term of up to 20 years. One day a policeman gained entrance to a private home in Georgia, and entered a private bedroom (opening the room's nearly closed door) where two men were so engaged, consensually. He arrested them, and they were charged with the crime of sodomy.

One of the men, Mr. Hardwick, challenged the law on constitutional grounds. He was represented before the United States Supreme Court by Professor Lawrence Tribe of Harvard Law School. The case, known as *Bowers v. Hardwick*, became a constitutional test of Georgia's law on the basis of the right of privacy. The case was fraught with the arguments of legislating according to outmoded societal norms against more enlightened views of private consensual relationships. The State of Georgia supported its law with 2000 years of history outlawing sodomy as a disgraceful practice, and most especially so when engaged between partners of the same sex. It seemed that Georgia was perhaps loosely arguing the concept of *stare decisis* in the Biblical sense. Professor Tribe rested his case upon the United States Constitution's anathema for intrusion of government into the privacy of the home of a private citizen who is not in breach of the peace. For whatever reason, at the time, the Court bought Georgia's argument, noting that the proscriptions against sodomy have ancient roots. Incredibly, Mr. Hardwick lost the case.

In 2003, 17 years later, along came a case called *Lawrence v. Texas*. In the Lawrence case, a remarkably similar Texas law against criminalizing sodomy was the subject again before the United States Supreme Court. According to case precedent — *stare decisis* — as argued by the Texas lawyers using the Bowers case as their basis, the Court would have also left the Texas law in place as well. Texas state lawyers relied on Bowers and argued that growing social tolerance was not sufficient to overcome well-settled law: "Four decades of gradual but incomplete decriminalization does not erase a history of one hundred and fifty years of universal reprobation." This time the argument of "ancient roots" did not carry the day, *stare decisis* notwithstanding. This time, the lawyers arguing against the state's law were the ones to prevail. The Court concluded that its decision in the Bowers case was just plain wrong. Here is why *stare decisis* did not work. The Court said:

"There has been no individual or societal reliance on *Bowers* of the sort that could counsel against overturning its holding once there are compelling reasons to do so. *Bowers* itself causes uncertainty, for the precedents before and after its issuance contradict its central holding. ". . . *Bowers* was not correct when it was decided, and it is not correct today. It ought not to remain binding precedent."

The Lawrence case is an example of how a case can be successfully argued against precedent and as a result, change the law. Note that the Court found no significant reliance by the courts, meaning ultimately by society, on the rule of law in Bowers, so as to make it an important precedent. In contrast, there had been decades of both individual and societal reliance on the *Roe v. Wade* decision. Such reliance upon a case as law renders it a dynamic precedent, and makes it more difficult for a Court to justify overturning it. Further, reliance was not the only factor working against the Texas sodomy law. The Court refused to apply Bowers as a precedent in the Texas case because it was persuaded that its prior decision in Bowers was patently not correct. Some decisions, in the face of critical thinking, simply cannot withstand the light of day. They may have been rendered on a faulty premise or assumption that subsequently comes to light.

Sometimes it takes another branch of government to overcome the power of *stare decisis*: a constitutional change, a legislative change, or an executive proclamation. A lawyer named Abraham Lincoln grappled with this option over the terrible rule of law that led to the *Dred Scott* decision. Lincoln opposed the United States Supreme Court's refusal to allow the emancipated slave, Dred Scott, to remain free when he was captured by slaveholders. Under the law of the land at that time, Scott was property, not a man but chattel, a rule of law that, though long gone, still haunts the history of this country today. Still, Lincoln understood the law of the day prevailed, and he understood what it would take to change it. At the time of the *Dred Scott* decision, Lincoln still hoped that a peaceful change could be wrought to eradicate slavery. In a speech on July 10, 1858, in Chicago, Lincoln said:

"What are the uses of decisions of courts? They have two uses. As rules of property they have two uses. First — they decide upon the question before the court. They decide in this case that Dred Scott is a slave. Nobody resists that. Not only that, but they say to everybody else, that persons standing just as Dred Scott stands is as he is. That is, they say that when a question comes up upon another person it will be so decided again, unless the court decides in another way, unless the court overrules its decision. Well, we mean to do what we can to have the court decide the other way. That is one thing we mean to try to do."

Lincoln understood that it takes some powerful persuasion to convince a court to overrule itself, but such is precisely the common law at work; the law evolves. Courts make the decisions, but lawyers bring the cases to the courts to make the arguments for and against the principles of law at work within a social context. This is what lawyers do. At the heart of the process of doing it best is critical thinking, giving the courts the argument, — the basis — to render the decision that is right and just; and by the way, the one you want for your client.

In Canada, the legal system is bijural, which is based on both English common law, and also, French civil law (like Louisiana), but much about the legal process in Canada and the United States works the same way. The process in both systems demands that lawyers exercise the kind of reasoning and intellectual abilities the LSAT purports to evaluate.

Law is an ever-evolving body of thought and decision that governs society from the privacy of homes to the public arena above the courthouse steps. It is a process that is subject to the push and pull of social policies and mores; hence the concept of "practicing" law. There is no finite mastery of the law; it will not be the same tomorrow that it is today. Simply stated, the practice of law is not an exact science. The demand for critical thinking in the legal profession never ceases.

The lawyer's work involves knowing, researching, understanding, interpreting, extrapolating and applying the law to specific factual situations; each one as unique as one human being is from another. Applying the law to specific, factual situations through analytical thinking, problem-solving, analogy, and communication of the resulting opinion or argument in a meaningful way, describes the lawyer's work. The lawyer not only needs to know the law, but also understand how courts interpret and apply the law, and how those same courts might be persuaded to take a new direction in the law.

It is important to think about the concept of precedent in the context of training yourself for the LSAT. The fundamental thought processes of critical thinking that are involved in researching and applying existing law, including most especially the case precedents of the common law and seeking to find new ways to apply them, are what the LSAT intends to be all about.

Studying for the legal profession and practicing as a lawyer require learning to think and reason in a specific way; one of understanding the law, and being able to push it a step beyond its current form when applying it to new situations. The LSAT is not about ascertaining what law school hopefuls know about the law or how to practice law; law school is supposed to teach them that when they get there. The LSAT is about assessing how students think and reason. LSAC designs the LSAT questions to test students' aptitude for the type of thinking utilized in the study and practice of law. You might scratch your head and question the validity of this premise at times, as you move through the LSAT practice tests and wonder how a logic Games matrix relates to interpreting the United States Constitution, but, to paraphrase Lincoln, "It is what it is."

9. Understand Law School Teaching Methodology

The LSAT's approach reflects that the teaching of law is a process; the development of a method of thinking and reasoning. Law schools primarily utilize the Socratic Method of teaching, which seeks to reveal a point through asking a series of questions rather than simply stating the bottom line answer, and then backing into an explanation of the answer. It is one of the oldest teaching methods we know, hearkening, as the name indicates, from Socrates' approach to teaching philosophy well over 2000 years ago. Socrates, an Athenian who lived in ancient Greece from about 469 to 399 B.C.E., employed critical reasoning and commitment to truth to challenge and teach his followers to think for themselves and to engage their minds to discover insight through the application of logic. In other words, Socrates sought to teach a method for finding truth through a process of independent thought and intellectual growth by questioning, rather than merely accepting and memorizing the statements of another. Socrates' approach would become the genesis and foundation of Western philosophical thought.

Insight to the Socratic Method of law is explained by the University of Chicago Law School on its excellent Web site, where it describes its 21st century Socratic approach in the law school classroom as follows:

"The day of the relentless Socratic professor who ended every sentence with a question mark is over. University of Chicago professors who rely on the Socratic Method today use participatory learning and discussions with a few students on whom they call (in some classrooms, randomly) to explore very difficult legal concepts and principles."

At its best this process is a cooperative exchange between teacher and class in the exploration of an issue; the goal being to teach students how to think like a lawyer, using, for example, critical thinking in the analysis of legal issues and extending understood concepts to new ones by use of the powerful analytical tool of analogy. Chicago Law further explains, "Socratic discourse requires participants to articulate, develop and defend positions that may at first be imperfectly defined intuitions. Lawyers are, first and foremost, problem solvers, and the primary task of law school is to equip our students with the tools they need to solve problems."

The ultimate goal of the Socratic Method is to instill a way of approaching legal issues and problems that works in any situation, not just specific cases or fact patterns. Within this framework law students study volumes of cases in which courts have reached a decision based on application of legal principles to specific facts. The cases are selected to illustrate types of law and legal reasoning in such fundamental areas as contracts, torts, evidence, family law, constitutional law, and criminal law. In the law school classroom students are challenged to identify the issues and legal principles of an adjudicated case and the analytical foundation of a court's reasoning in reaching its conclusion, and from there, to grasp the art of applying the court's reasoning to other case applications. It is with the demands of this process in mind that law schools consider which new applicants exhibit the best potential for success.

Law schools may consider a variety of criteria in their selection of first-year students, but the ones most universally applied are the student's GPA in undergraduate and graduate school, LSAT score, and demonstrated writing ability. Of these, for good or for ill, as noted in the statistics of law school rankings, it is the LSAT score that ordinarily carries the most weight. The reason most often given for the LSAT score's importance rests on the fact that law school applicants come from a variety of colleges and universities. These various institutions inherently differ in their grading standards, coursework, and teaching methodology. The LSAT is viewed as the objective leveler of the playing field for applicants from diverse places and disciplines. Considering the principles of legal analysis and the cognitive demands of the legal profession, the LSAT purports to sample a person's ability to quickly read, comprehend, and analyze complexities in a logical manner, draw analogies and inferences, identify fallacies, avoid the traps of linear thinking, and reach a relevant conclusion.

Once you are accepted in law school, it will no longer matter how high you scored on the LSAT; nor are you likely to ever again encounter the type of questions that you faced on the LSAT. What you will encounter is the need for the type of skills the LSAT purports to measure. There will be other tests ahead of you, ultimately the Biggest Bear of all tests: the Bar Examination. First, though, you have to get accepted into law school. You can hone your skills and prepare yourself to improve your LSAT score, in turn broadening your choices of schools and opportunities and bolstering your readiness for the demands of the study of law.

10. Pay Attention to the Law School Admissions Council

The LSAT is created, administered, scored, and reported to law schools by LSAC, a nonprofit corporation whose members consist of over 200 American and Canadian law schools. LSAC provides various types of LSAT preparation materials, including actual full-length tests previously given to law school applicants.

You will find a plethora of LSAT preparatory sources available on the market, many of them excellent. Simply enter "LSAT" in your favorite Internet search engine and an amazing number of possibilities will come up in your search results. Regardless of the resources that beckon you, do not overlook advice and counsel from the creators of the test. Although it often may seem to be obscure, there is a method to their madness.

11. Be Prepared for Multiple Timed Sections

The LSAT is not administered in a single time block that gives you a half-day to complete it. In reality it is six tests administered back-to-back. The LSAT is divided into five timed sections, 35 minutes each, of standardized multiple-choice questions divided into sections called Reading Comprehension, Logical Reasoning (Arguments), and Analytical Reasoning (Games). The test questions utilize a diverse selection of five verbal and analytical sections. Four of the sections will count toward your score. The fifth multiple-choice section is the Experimental section. It is not scored, and varies from test to test. It may be the first section of the test or appear anywhere else. The last and sixth section is the Writing Sample portion of the test, which is not scored but is sent to the law schools who receive your LSAT test results.

12. Do Not Waste Time Worrying about the Experimental Section

If there is a section on the LSAT that surprises you even after all your months of preparation, it may well be LSAC's Experimental section. This is the non-scored section of newly-constructed questions which LSAC analyzes in the test results to decide how it will design questions that will be scored on the future LSAT editions. While you might take an educated guess at which is the Experimental section, in point of fact, you will not know for sure during the test which section is this non-scored variable, and it will be a waste of your concentration and energy to try to figure it out while taking the test.

13. Understand the LSAT's Format

Understanding the purpose and structure of the LSAT will assist you in understanding the broad context and mindset of the questions. That understanding may be the key to choosing the best answer to a question when there seems to be either no right answer or more than one right answer.

Each of the LSAT's 35-minute multiple-choice sections commonly ranges from 24 to 27 questions. These sections may appear in any order per test booklet, but will consist of the following:

- Reading Comprehension

- Analytical Reasoning/Games

- Logical Reasoning/Arguments

- Logical Reasoning/Arguments

- Experimental Section (may be any of above subjects)

- The Writing Sample is conducted in its own 35-minute time slot.

The LSAT questions appear in the LSAT test booklet with a separate answer sheet that contains bubbles labeled A-B-C-D-E for each numbered question. You indicate your answer response to a question by fully filling in the corresponding bubble for that question with a No. 2 pencil (HB pencil in Canada). This is often described as "bubbling your answer."

It is important to know that the LSAT does not order its questions according to level of difficulty; such as, the easiest first and the hardest last in each section. You will need to gauge each question on its own merits. All questions are equal in weight and value; the answer to an easy question is worth as much as the answer to a hard one. A guess is better than leaving a question unanswered. An educated guess is better than a random guess.

14. Prepare for Arguments

Logical Reasoning - Arguments

One of your essential preparatory tools is the practice test. Many test preparatory services, including LSAC's official published materials, offer sample test questions for practice with explanations of the correct and incorrect answers. Actual past LSAT tests are available for practice. As you work through your early practice tests, you will recognize that about 50 percent of the LSAT is comprised of Argument-style questions, set forth in two Logical Reasoning/Argument sections.

LSAC defines Arguments as "short, self-contained sets of statements that present evidence and draw a conclusion on the basis of that evidence." Here is a simple example of this type of Argument.

The company's layoff policy is processed solely on the basis of seniority. Lucy has been employed for five years. Damian has been employed for four years and seven months. Therefore, if the company proceeds with layoffs, Damian will be laid off before Lucy.

In this Argument, three facts, or evidence, are stated in the first three sentences. These facts are premises: (1) the company's layoff policy – seniority; (2) Lucy employed five years; (3) Damian employed four years and seven months – five months less than Lucy. These three premises support the conclusion that is stated in the last sentence, which is that Damian will be laid off before Lucy.

15. Understand Argument Structure

The following imaginary example demonstrates a two-tiered Logical Reasoning/Argument structure.

Dr. Ingenold Smythe is a well-known expert in forensic psychology who has testified in over 500 cases on the side of the prosecution opposing the defense of not guilty by reason of insanity. The overwhelming majority of the cases in which Dr. Smythe has given evidence resulted in convictions. Therefore, Dr. Smythe's opinion is exceedingly persuasive with juries. The prosecution has engaged Dr. Smythe as an expert for the prosecution in the murder indictment of Grayson Greer. Accordingly, it is not likely that Greer's insanity defense will save him from the gas chamber.

There are three initial premises in this example: (1) Dr. Smythe's expertise in forensic psychology; (2) the large number of trials in which he has testified; and (3) the prosecution won in most of those cases in which Smythe testified. These premises lead to an intermediate conclusion that Dr. Smythe's testimony is persuasive with juries. From that intermediate conclusion, the Logical Reasoning/Argument adds the additional premise that the prosecution in the Greer case has hired Dr. Smythe. This fact in conjunction with the conclusion of Dr. Smythe's clout with juries leads to the main conclusion of the passage, which is that Greer will be convicted.

16. Recognize Argument Signposts

Each Argument passage in the LSAT Logical Reasoning/ Argument section can be parsed into premises (purely factual statements), and intermediate and/or main conclusions. You can distinguish the difference by noting that the premises are simply stated facts without them being related to other statements to support them. There is no discussion about them to justify that they are true, as they are plainly stated as truths. In the above example about Dr. Smythe in the Greer case, the stated facts are clear.

Premise and Counter Premise Signposts

There are certain words often employed on the LSAT that are premise words or signposts. Other words are counter premise words or phrases, which indicate a juxtaposition of opposite, or counter, ideas. Some of the most often-used premise and counter premise signposts are:

Premise Signposts:

- Since

- Evidences

- May be derived from

- Assume

- Suppose

- Imagine

- Consider

- Visualize

- Suggest

Counter Premise Signposts:

- But

- However

- Even though

- Though

- Except

- Despite

- Regardless

- Although

- Notwithstanding

- Nonetheless

- Nevertheless

Conclusion Signposts

In the above example about Dr. Smythe and the Greer case, the intermediate conclusion is identifiable by the word "therefore" at the beginning of the sentence stating that Dr. Smythe is persuasive with juries. The main conclusion is introduced with the word "accordingly." Thus, certain words signal "Here comes a conclusion." These words include:

- So

- Therefore

- As a result

- Means

- Tells us

- Proves

- Evidences

- Thus

- Signals

- Signifies

- This leads to

- Consequently

- It follows

- Implies

- Hence

- Accordingly

- Means that

- For this reason

- For that reason

- Conclude

Further, words such as "likely," "probably," "makes possible," "predicts," are often found in conclusion statements. Be careful, though, that you do not just seize on words like these and assume they identify the main conclusion of the passage. As the Dr. Smythe example demonstrates, there can be more than one conclusion in a passage, only one of which is the main conclusion, and the conclusions may fall in any order, depending on how the passage is structured; this is the beauty and the beast of the English language. There are many ways to say the same thing, and have them appear to be different from each other. There is no bright line between intermediate conclusion signposts and main conclusion signposts. Critical thinking skills are necessary to unmask these seeming differences and put them in their place.

Though the most common structure of an Argument passage is premise followed by conclusion, there is no specific template, no required order that will always appear in an LSAT passage. The passage could start with a conclusion and proceed to support it. The conclusion could be buried in the premise statement. In analyzing the Argument passage, it is important to pay attention to what each statement contributes to the Argument. Ask yourself: is it an opinion based on other statements or is it a stand-alone fact recited to support the conclusion?

The Logical Reasoning/Argument questions on the LSAT do not anticipate or require that you know formal terms of logic, but LSAC cautions that they do require "that you possess, at a minimum, a college-level understanding of widely used concepts such as argument, premise, assumption, and conclusion." Also, be careful not to allow your own preconceptions about the facts presented in the question to intrude or confuse your evaluation of each question.

17. Work on Argument Analytical Skills

The Logical Reasoning/Argument questions bring into play several skills involving logic and critical thinking. The LSAT experts surveyed agree that these skills include the following, any of which may be employed in specific test questions:

- Identifying and applying the writer's beliefs stated in the passage

- Identifying the main point or issue of a dispute

- Recognizing how additional evidence affects the writer's conclusion

- Recognizing any assumptions underlying the writer's statements

- Recognizing fallacies in the writer's conclusions, such as false or missing assumptions

- Identifying the writer's reasoning

- Separating fact from opinion.

Some of these could be interrelated in a question. For example, it will be necessary to identify the writer's reasoning chain in order to recognize fallacies in the conclusion.

18. Stay Within the Four Corners of the Question's Statements

The following is a hypothetical, generic example of a Logical Reasoning, or Argument-style question, patterned after the type of questions used on past LSATs.

Heart disease is lower in incidence in Italy than in the United States. Studies show that Italians consume more olive oil than Americans. Therefore, consumption of olive oil prevents heart disease.

Question: Which of the following statements, if true, would refute the conclusion in this passage?

(A) More Americans than Italians die of heart attacks.

(B) Americans who have heart disease drink more wine than Italians.

(C) Americans who have heart disease are found to consume higher quantities of olive oil than Americans who do not suffer heart disease.

(D) Some Americans who consume a lot of olive oil are of Italian heritage.

(E) Both Americans and Italians are prone to heart disease.

You must assume the passage and evidence it presents to be true. Do not be distracted by whether you think any of its statements are true or false in the real world. The question requires you to consider the question's statements (the premises), and its conclusion — that olive oil in the human diet prevents heart disease — and determine how the statements in each of the possible answers, also presumed to be true, relate to or affect that conclusion. The question also calls for an understanding of the word "refute," which means here to negate the validity of the conclusion.

Answer (A) truly supports the conclusion. The statement that more Americans than Italians die of heart attacks is consistent with the statement that more Americans than Italians have heart disease. Therefore, (A) does not provide evidence that refutes the conclusion and can be quickly eliminated as a possible correct answer.

Answer (B) neither supports nor discredits the conclusion about olive oil because it talks about wine consumption. It is a statement unrelated to the premise of olive oil consumption. Therefore, it does not refute the conclusion and cannot be correct.

Likewise, answer (D) contributes nothing to the connection of olive oil to reducing heart disease, because it links Americans' consumption of olive oil to being Italian with no reference to heart disease. Therefore, it does not relate to the conclusion about heart disease. At most, it is consistent with the notion of Italians consuming more olive oil and adds nothing new to the facts.

Answer (E) states a conclusion about Americans and Italians having heart disease. It relates to the passage only in that the passage compares heart disease incidence between Americans and Italians. (E) does not state anything that refutes, or supports for that matter, the author's conclusion about olive oil's prevention of heart disease. Therefore, (E) is not relevant to the question asked either.

Answer (C), on the other hand, provides evidence contrary to the author's conclusion because it states that another study shows a higher incidence of heart disease in higher consumers of olive oil. This study adds a contradictory fact. As a result, when added as an additional premise, (C) directly refutes the logic of the conclusion that olive oil consumption prevents heart disease. (C) is the correct answer.

The above hypothetical question tests the skill of recognizing how additional evidence affects the writer's conclusion.

For the above question on the LSAT, you would fill in the bubble for "C" for the corresponding question number on the separate answer sheet.

19. Prepare for Games

Analytical Reasoning – Games

The LSAT Analytical Reasoning/Games section by and large presents scenarios describing relationships of a group, and then poses selections of conclusions to choose as correct — or not — based on the rules of those relationships. LSAC defines this section of the LSAT as follows:

"Analytical reasoning items are designed to measure your ability to understand a structure of relationships and to draw logical conclusions about the structure. You are tasked to make deductions from a set of statements, rules, or conditions that describe relationships among entities such as persons, places, things, or events."

Thus, the Analytical Reasoning/Games questions require you to understand spatial relationships and deduce the answer to a question dependent upon those relationships. Simply stated, these are logic games. The following is a relatively simple hypothetical, generic illustration of an Analytical Reasoning/Games type question:

Jane, Joe, Jeremy, Rose and Rita are going to carpool to a football game in three cars. Jane has to drive her own car. Jane will not drive alone. Jane cannot ride with Rita. Rita cannot ride with Rose. Jeremy is the only one who cannot drive. Rose and Joe cannot ride with Jeremy. Jane cannot ride with Joe.

Question: Who is driving Jeremy?

(A) Joe

(B) Jane

(C) Rita

(D) Rita or Jane

(E) Rose

Your starting point is five people who have to fit into three cars according to the limitations of who can ride with whom and who can and cannot drive. It is a grouping Game.

20. What Does the Question Ask

Before thinking of all the possible combinations, consider exactly what it is the question asks; in this case, "Who is driving Jeremy?" The starting point is with whom Jeremy can share a car. Diagramming the relationships, using three boxes for the cars, can be helpful; the LSAT does not allow you to bring in scrap paper, but you can use the blank spaces in the test booklet. You know that one car belongs to Jane because the rules require that she has to drive, so your starting diagram might look like this; now you can use the diagram to play with the combinations of relationships defined in the question.

Jane's car	Car No. 2	Car No. 3

Answer (A) says Jeremy rides with Joe. Does that work? Easy. The facts tell you that Jeremy cannot be in the same car with Joe. (A) can be eliminated immediately as a possible answer. Similarly, answer (E) is quickly eliminated because the rules tell you that Jeremy cannot be in the same car with Rose either.

The remaining choices of answers state that Jeremy rides with (B) Jane, (C) Rita, or (D) either Jane or Rita. As noted in eliminating (A) and (E), the facts further tell you that Jeremy cannot be in the same car with Rose or Joe. That leaves Rita or Jane to drive Jeremy. At this point, neither (B), (C), nor (D) can be eliminated.

You also know for sure that Jane is one of the drivers and that she has to have someone with her. It cannot be Rita or Joe. So, if Jeremy is in Jane's car, do the rest of the people fit into the other cars within the rules of their relationships? Put Jeremy in Jane's car and see if the others will fit in the other two cars without crossing up one of the rules. Rose cannot ride with Rita, but she can with Joe. Rita can drive by herself.

Jane's car Jeremy	Car No. 2 Rita	Car No. 3 Joe Rose

So, answer (B) is correct. But wait -- what about (D) – can Jeremy also ride with Rita in the alternative? If Rita is driving Jeremy, will the others be able to ride in the other two cars? Fill in the names accordingly and test them against the description of the relationships.

Jane's car Rose	Rita's Car Jeremy	Joe's Car

Yes, it works. If Jeremy rides with Rita, then Rose can ride with Jane (so that Jane is not alone), Joe can drive by himself, and everyone gets to the game. Thus, while (B) and (C) are each true, the best and therefore correct answer to the question is (D). Jeremy can ride with either Rita or Jane. By diagramming it, you can more easily visualize the facts, place the people into the various cars, and test the arrangement against the relationship rules described in the question.

21. The First "Right" Answer May Not be the Best Answer

The previous carpool example illustrates the necessity of not only working out the answer to the question but also considering all the possible answers provided with the question. If you read the question and turned to solve it but stopped as soon as you determined one of Jeremy's drivers, you might pick (B) or (C) in haste, as either might be the first driver you conclude can drive Jeremy. On the other hand, you may fall into the trap of assuming that only one arrangement will work and that (D) is a red herring. Diagramming is often indispensable for solving the logic Games.

22. Note the Type of Game in Play

As mentioned, the carpool game is an example of a grouping Game. Two other types of Games frequently encountered on the LSAT are ordering Games and assignment Games. An ordering Game requires you to organize several items, in a row or around a table such as a circle or rectangle, according to rules limiting who is able to sit next to whom; or it might ask you to fill in a blank in the ordering based on where you are told some of the players are located. A typical question is a group standing in line for something, such as waiting to buy tickets. Example:

Angela, Adam, Faye, Ray, George and Georgia are in line for tickets to the Metallica concert.

- Faye is second in line and is not next to Angela.

- Adam is immediately in front of Georgia.

- Ray is not first.

Question: Which one of the following people must be first in line?

(A) Faye

(B) Georgia

(C) Adam

(D) George

(E) Angela

All the test prep experts recommend that diagramming is the key to getting through the Games section of the LSAT. Especially if you are a visual person, it may help to test this question's possible answers by quickly setting up a diagram such as the following, representing the line of six people and placing Faye, whose place is the one specifically set by the rules.

1.	2. Faye	3.	4.	5.	6.

You have six people, so six places in line. Faye is second in line, so first is immediately in front of Faye. Of the answers given to the question, who can be first in line according to the rules?

Not Faye, because she is already in 2nd place, not first. Thus answer (A) is eliminated.

Not Angela, because she cannot be next to Faye and first place is next to Faye. So, answer (E) is eliminated.

Not Adam, because he is immediately in front of Georgia. To be in first place, he would have to be immediately front of Faye. So (C) is also eliminated.

Not Georgia because if Adam is immediately in front of her, then she is immediately behind Adam, who is behind Faye, which also puts Georgia behind Faye. Therefore, answer (B) is also eliminated.

By a fairly quick process of elimination, the correct answer has to be (D) George. He is the only one left of the "possibles."

Note that to solve this Game question, you do not have to figure out the exact order of people behind of Faye. You only need to recognize who, of the answers provided, cannot be in front of her in first place. A trap of this question would be to try to line up everyone in order before looking to the answers of the question, and thereby waste precious time.

The following is the third example of Games commonly found in the Analytical Reasoning/Games section of the LSAT — the assignment Game. In these Games, characteristics are assigned to people or items, such as a color of shirt, type of hat, or a schedule of when people work. Based on these rules, you are asked to determine who is where. Consider the following hypothetical example:

Ye Olde Yarne Shoppe employs five clerks, one for each weekday, Monday through Friday. The owner, Zeta, works on Saturdays. The Shoppe is closed on Sundays. The five weekday clerks are: Anna, Barb, Candy, Grace, and Zena. Each works alone on her assigned day.

- Anna will work only on Tuesday or Thursday.

- Barb will not work on Monday or Wednesday.

- Candy only works on Friday.

- Grace and Zena do not work on consecutive days.

Question: Which one of the following is a possible work schedule, Monday through Friday?

(A) Zena, Barb, Anna, Grace, Candy

(B) Grace, Anna, Barb, Zena, Candy

(C) Zena, Anna, Candy, Barb, Grace

(D) Zena, Anna, Grace, Barb, Candy

(E) Grace, Zena, Barb, Anna, Candy

Diagramming this one is easily done with five boxes, one for each day of the week. Then note how people could line up according to the rules. You do not care about Zeta the owner, because she is isolated on Saturday and none of the five clerks work on Saturday.

M	T	W	Th	F
G or Z	A or B	G or Z	A or B	C

The diagram shows each person on a day she can work, and Grace and Zena are placed on nonconsecutive days. First, fill in Candy (C) because you know she works only on Friday. That eliminates Friday as a possible day for any of the others. Anna only works on Tuesday or Thursday, so "A" is placed on both those days. Barb will not work on Mondays or Wednesdays, and because of Candy's Friday assignment, that leaves either Tuesday or Thursday for Barb. So "A or B" fit on Tuesdays and Thursdays. That leaves Grace or Zena each as possibles for Monday and

Wednesday because those two days are left open that are not consecutive days.

Now you can test the possible answers given for the question, according to the rules shown above. (A) is eliminated because Anna does not work on Wednesday. (B) is eliminated because Barb does not work on Wednesday. (C) does not work either because Candy only works on Friday and therefore cannot be scheduled on Wednesday. (D) works, because it places everyone is on a day she can work, and Grace and Zena are not placed on consecutive days. As a result, (D) is the correct answer. At this point, if you are confident in your diagram of the rules, move on to the next question. You can quickly verify (D) is correct, though, by simply looking at (E) and noting that it has Grace and Zena scheduled on consecutive days.

Note that in the spatial rules of these examples, words like "consecutive" and "immediately behind" are utilized. If a rule does not use a modifier like "immediately" in an example like this, be careful you do not unthinkingly add the condition of "immediately" or "consecutive" in your mind. A rule may state that A is in front of B. If there is more than one space in front of B, A could be in any of them, not necessarily in the space immediately adjacent to B. The rules stated in each Analytical Reasoning/Game must be read literally and exactly. Do not add more limits than are expressly stated.

23. Prepare for Reading Comprehension

LSAC defines the Reading Comprehension section of the LSAT as, "intended to assess your ability to read, with understanding and insight, passages comparable in terms of level of language and complexity to materials you are likely to have to deal with in the study of law." This section of the LSAT normally presents passages of varying lengths and levels of factual complexity, each followed by a question or questions designed to probe your understanding of the passage you have just read. The questions may ask you to identify the main theme or point of the passage, draw a conclusion or inference based on the passage, identify a correct statement of fact based on the passage, recognize a fallacy, or draw distinctions.

As if the challenges of decoding one passage were not enough, in 2007, LSAC added a new dimension to the Reading Comprehension section of the LSAT -- comparative reading questions. These questions will provide two narrative texts for a problem and set up questions requiring you to compare them in various ways.

24. Read Critically

In Reading Comprehension, the LSAT demands that you read critically alert for the writer's (writers on the comparative reading problems) theme, purpose, premise, conclusions, and even analytical flaws. LSAC explains that the Reading Comprehension section includes questions that:

- Require recognition of analogous patterns of facts in different situations.

- Derive conclusions or inferences from the writer's context.

- Explore the writer's attitude or agenda.

- Require you to determine the effect of additional information on the writer's thoughts, conclusion or opinion.

25. Learn to Read Quickly

The Reading Comprehension section's time limit demands a quick grasp of the text and questions. You have less than two minutes (normally approximately 1.4 minutes) per question, and that time limit includes reading and analyzing text, and also the questions themselves. If you tend to be a slow reader, you might consider including a speed reading course as a component of your preparation for the LSAT. Speed reading in and of itself will not be your savior, because true speed reading style is a scanning technique that could lead some individuals to miss important details. Nevertheless, speed reading used in conjunction with other LSAT preparation aids might be a useful tool to increase your reading rate, especially if your slow reading rate is tied to a compulsive word-by-word approach. Also, an improved reading rate will be immensely helpful in law school. Few students need to do more reading in a sustained, compressed time period than first-year law students.

26. Do Not Sacrifice Focus for Speed

The ultimate challenge of the LSAT is concentration counterpoised with speed. The test presses you to read and absorb concepts, and quickly interpret them according to the demands of the questions. Only practice will help you find the balance between these challenges.

The following hypothetical problem is an example of the type of Reading Comprehension passage you might encounter on the LSAT:

Reading Comprehension Passage

"Mark Twain's *Huckleberry Finn* depicts Arkansas as a social backwater. The one-horse towns that Huck Finn encounters along the Mississippi are collections of the crudest sort of humanity; one characterized by laziness, insensitivity, stubbornness, and sadism. Huck sums them up well when he calls them 'a mighty ornery lot.' The men take their greatest pleasure in watching a dogfight, or putting turpentine on a dog and setting fire to it. If a stray welfare worker were to step among them to reform their ways, they would be happy to tar and feather the poor bastard as payment for his trouble, just as they do to Twain's 'poor friendless cast-out women.'

"This is not an audience that will appreciate the literary attributes of the Duke's Shakespearean road show. They need to be enticed by the promise of something more basic. The Duke employs artful advertising psychology to attract them to the show. These people who seek their pleasures in torturing dogs and the titillating details of a killing in town require the physically exciting, the stimulation of senses, not intellect. Nor is this anticipation of vulgar pleasure limited to the lower classes. Twain illustrates their inherent sadism and enthusiasm for fighting in the Arkansas aristocrats' feud. Just like their lowly counterparts on the social scale, these relatively well off Arkansans would not shy from the promise of a lewd sideshow.

"Twain presents the coarse backwoods society in the moral shadow of a Puritan heritage, self-righteous in its judgment of others but certain in the entertainment value of a show unfit for the eyes of innocent women and children. Not a man in town will miss a show so tantalizingly publicized. It may not be morally acceptable, but it is fun, and for men only."

Question No. 1: The author's main purpose in this writing is:

(A) Commentary of men in society

(B) Literary criticism of the writings of Mark Twain

(C) Hypocrisy of the so-called upper classes

(D) Women should be able to attend lewd shows if they want to

(E) The author of this passage does not like Arkansas.

Question No. 2: Which of the following is the best statement of the writer's theme in this passage?

(A) *Huckleberry Finn* is about life on the Mississippi River.

(B) Twain describes the Arkansas river town in *Huckleberry Finn* as a misogynistic sadistic social group.

(C) People who kill other people cannot appreciate Shakespeare.

(D) The Duke does not believe in truth in advertising.

(E) It is tough to be a woman in Arkansas.

Question No. 3: Which of the following statements is most likely to be true from the viewpoint of the writer of this passage?

(A) Mark Twain held a deep admiration for the backwoods lifestyle of the Mississippi pioneers.

(B) Mark Twain used humor and irony to reveal the low status and unfair treatment of women in the Arkansas culture.

(C) *Huckleberry Finn* was the pulp fiction of its day.

(D) The illiterate deserve what they get.

(E) Shakespeare had no place and no hope of appreciation in a backwater river town of nineteenth century Arkansas.

Question No. 4: Which of the following best describes the writer's description of the Arkansans' social structure as depicted in Huckleberry Finn?

(A) Matriarchy

(B) Anarchy

(C) Patriarchy

(D) Polyglot

(E) Democracy

Commentary: There is a lot of food for thought in the passage about noted author Mark Twain's writing. It is important on the LSAT to keep focused and read the question. Question No. 1 asks you to identify the purpose of the writing. It is not a question about the passage's content specifically or the author's opinions. Focusing on the writer's purpose the answer must be (B), literary criticism, which is a written interpretation and commentary on literature. What is wrong with the other answers? (A) is alluring because the passage certainly contains a negative description of a male-dominated social group; although the author of the passage is writing interpretively about Mark Twain's writing as commentary as opposed to the author's own beliefs. Further, (A) is too broad a statement for the scope of the passage you are given.

On the other hand, (C) is too narrow a statement. It simply refers to one piece of information that is part of Mark Twain's story and which provides a springboard for the discussion of the Arkansas river town. Similarly, (D) is simply a conclusory, interpretive statement about the Duke, obviously one of Twain's characters, which you could discern from context even if you had not read *Huckleberry Finn*. (D) is not responsive to the question for a couple of reasons. One is that there is no factual basis for it in the passage. Most of the passage is devoted to the social group of the town, for which the Duke's road show is a vehicle for describing Twain's view of the town's citizenry. Also, (E) is a conclusory opinion that overly generalizes at best as it relates to the passage. (E) evidences a big leap from a narrative about Arkansas as depicted in Mark Twain's story to a broad statement about how the writer, allegedly, personally feels about the state of Arkansas. There are no statements in the passage that support such a conclusion about the writer's personal views. (D) and (E) should be the first two answers you eliminated in considering this question.

Question No. 2 asks about a different concept — theme, rather than purpose. A theme in writing is the author's unifying idea or recurrent element that is central to the writing. Here the writer is a literary critic writing about Mark Twain's *Huckleberry Finn*; and, is interpreting a piece of Mark Twain's writing as a social commentary on a male-dominated social group that is not high on the literacy scale. Understanding that the theme is the central subject matter of the writing, you should readily observe that (C), (D), and (E) are easily eliminated. (C) and (E) are simple, narrow statements that are tangential to most of the passage. Furthermore, (D) is not even factually supported by any statement in the passage. There is no mention that the Duke lied outright about his show.

Having quickly eliminated three answer choices, you are left with (A), a broad summary that fits the facts of the passage, or (B), which is a more specific statement. Of the two, (B) is the one that more closely relates to statements emphasized in the passage, most of which is devoted to describing how men crudely dominate the social structure and the sadistic behavior they exhibit in the Arkansas river town. Are there clues in the passage that the author sees the men to be misogynistic; that is, disrespecters, even haters, of women? Certainly. The writer points out that they enjoy the past time of tarring and feathering certain unfortunate women and employ a double standard as to what is suitable for women as opposed to men. Of the choices presented for the author's theme in this passage, (B) is the best, and therefore, the correct answer.

Question No. 3 asks you to interpret the writer's viewpoint based on your reading of the passage. This type of question probes your ability to translate a deeper understanding of the passage to the LSAT answer choices. As will be the case with most LSAT questions, there are at least two answers that you can quickly eliminate — (A) and (C). Nothing in the passage suggests that Twain was lauding the citizens of this particular Arkansas river town; nor does the passage suggest that the writer was passing it off as pulp fiction. To the contrary, the passage has the tenor of a more serious, literary commentary. Of the remaining three there is not much of a contest either. The emphasis on the plight of women in the passage makes (B) the obvious choice, especially with (D) and (E) being such weak possibilities. There is no comment in the passage about the illiterate being "deserving" of ill fate. As to Shakespeare, the Duke actually is presenting the show, and whether it was appreciated is not mentioned in the passage, and therefore, not pertinent to the writer's theme.

Question No. 4 is an example of a way the LSAT might slip in vocabulary with an interpretation question. If you understand that patriarchy is a male-dominated culture, you will know that the answer is (C); a matriarchy is a female-dominated social group. A polyglot is someone who can speak, read, write, and understand other languages beside his or her native tongue. In a democracy, each person has equal standing.

27. Do Not Totally Discount the Writing Sample

One LSAT expert, The Princeton Review, describes the Writing Sample section as "inconsequential." This is not an aberrational opinion, as many preparatory sources spend little, if any time at all, on this portion of the LSAT. Conversely, others — this writer included — disagree with the notion that you can safely omit work on the Writing Sample from your LSAT preparation plan. The purpose of the Writing Sample is to demonstrate your ability to express yourself clearly, organize and present ideas, recognize the subject presented, and stay on topic. The Writing Sample further will demonstrate your grasp of the mechanics of writing; from constructing a coherent sentence to demonstrating use of correct grammar, punctuation, diction, and spelling.

About this section of its test, LSAC cautions, "how well you write is more important than how much you write." Some law schools may look at the Writing Sample as a tiebreaker in making their admissions selections between closely-qualified candidates. Law school admissions consultant, Ann Levin (included in this book's Case Studies), points out that a well-done Writing Sample may be especially helpful for applicants for whom English is a second language. Admissions officers may compare the Writing Sample to the applicant's personal statement on the law school application to get a sense of whether the personal statement was written by the applicant.

The possibility of such a comparison exists for every applicant because law schools know and understand that applicants are likely to seek help in writing their personal statements. Such assistance is to be expected on such an important document as a law school application. Even applicants who seek no help, though, are not restricted to a 35-minute time limit to write it. They have time to polish it, and a creditable result is predictable accordingly. The Writing Sample provides a snapshot of reasoning and ability to communicate quickly and well. Although the Writing Sample does not impact your numerical LSAT score, it is unwise to completely disregard it in your preparation. It is a part of the test for a reason.

28. Repeat the Test if Necessary

There is no limit to how many times you can take the LSAT. Until recently if you took the LSAT more than once, your scores, most likely, would have been averaged together for one composite score, diluting the value of the higher score. In 2006 the ABA began requiring law schools to report the highest score of each applicant. The secondary benefit of this requirement has been for many law schools to cease averaging multiple scores. It may be worthwhile to retake the LSAT if your first score is lower than you need for your target law schools. If you are in this situation, do prepare for that second test.

29. Do Not Plan to Wing It! Prepare for the LSAT

It should be apparent to you by now that the best approach to improving your LSAT score is to seriously prepare for taking the test. Preparation should not be approached as a rote exercise of taking practice tests over and over. Rather, optimize your test score with a plan of attack designed especially for you. Intelligent preparation for the LSAT truly is quality over quantity.

Where do you start? There are many help systems on the market: books, computerized programs, practice tests, classroom programs, and individual gurus. Comprehensive professional prep services, like Kaplan, offer free introductory presentations or a sample class that demonstrates their LSAT approach. There are certain fundamental principles of preparation that are advisable for everyone. Beyond those, you need to determine the approach – or combination of approaches – that best meets your unique needs, and then use it.

30. Understand Your Resources and Limitations

Do not be bewildered by the plethora of resources available on the market. The fact that there is such a bountiful menu of preparatory options means that you should be able to put together an effective individualized program. The following considerations should affect your choice of resources and preparation plan.

- How much time do you have to prepare? Months, Weeks, Days?

- Are you a self-starter or do you work better within an externally imposed structure?

- What is the level of your pre-preparatory LSAT skills?

- Having taken a sounding of your comfort with the LSAT questions, which type of help will best serve your needs?

- How much money can you afford to spend?

Your answers to these questions will guide you in developing a meaningful preparatory plan. Start with an assessment of your skills – your strengths and weaknesses – and design your preparation plan accordingly. Whatever you decide to map out for a plan, be as complete as possible, and put it in writing.

2

Assessing Your LSAT Acumen

31. Introduce Yourself to the LSAT — Initial Self-Assessment

Before leaping at random into the bewildering number of resources available for LSAT preparation, take an initial sounding for yourself. After your own initial self-assessment, you should have a better idea of your strengths and weaknesses for the LSAT challenge. You should be able to evaluate the numerous resources available to you for your preparation, and choose those that will optimize your preparation time, and ultimately, your LSAT score.

The LSAT is purposely designed to be unique unto itself. In many respects it will not mimic other tests you have taken before. Start by taking a sample LSAT, or sample LSAT sections. Before investing money in books and online programs that contain practice tests, utilize the many free resources available online and in the library. After your initial foray into the test, you should survey the type of paid resources that will best fit your preparation needs, schedule, and budget.

32. Sample the Test

The best place to start is a "dry run." Several of the LSAT preparation services offer free test sections to get you started. While you will find many of these by entering "LSAT" into your Web search engine, some current resources are:

- **www.lsac.org/pdfs/test.pdf** — (LSAC)

- **www.testpreview.com** — (test sample modules)

- **www.princetonreview.com** — (free LSAT demo online)

- **www.lsatprepcourse.com** — (35-minute critical reasoning section)

- **www.west.net/~stewart/lsat/** — (mini tests)

- **www.kaptest.com/Kaplan/Article/Law/LSAT** — (practice test)

Hard copy test volumes containing full sample tests also may be available in the reference section of the public or college library.

You do not necessarily need to begin with a full-blown, real, past test, although you could. At this point you need to acquire an understanding of how the various types of LSAT questions work, and how they challenge you in particular. Whether beginning with a complete test or sample sections, remember that on the timed LSAT multiple-choice sections, you have approximately

1.4 minutes per question. Given that the test sections are designed not to be readily finished in the time allowed, you cannot afford to spend too much time on any one question. If you find yourself doing this, or simply losing track of time passing, you will have an indicator that you need to work on pacing yourself through the questions. In the discussion of question types earlier in the book, it was noted that there are test-taking techniques to help you improve this skill.

33. Evaluate Your Strengths & Weaknesses

You may find that your natural skills are more attuned to some types of questions on the LSAT than others. Use the initial practice questions to familiarize yourself with the type and structure of the test questions, and reveal where you are going to need the most practice or problem analysis. Design your preparation program accordingly. Having oriented yourself with sample questions, honestly evaluate your "rough spots" in types of questions, concepts, your own thinking habits or patterns, and timing. Focus less on your early practice scores of right and wrong answers than on the type of questions or test sections which cause you the most struggles. Those are the areas to emphasize in your preparation plan, and for which you will benefit from expert help.

As you work through the test questions mark those that most trouble you. Then, as you check through your answers, analyze each question as to why the correct answer is correct — even if you got it right initially. Some people become quite frustrated in this early process. It is easy to become sidetracked in arguing, or fighting, against the answer LSAC deems to be correct. The reality is your indignation will be better channeled into figuring out why the correct answer is the best answer.

34. Do Not Let Yourself Be Intimidated

On their first brush with the LSAT questions, some people are inclined to throw up their hands, saying, "There is no way I can prepare for THIS!" This is not true; you can prepare for anything. You can take the LSAT apart and put it back together again over the course of your preparation time. The preparatory materials, and counselors you choose should provide you explanations of how the LSAT questions are constructed, and the approaches effective for you to solve them quickly. For example, *The Official LSAT SuperPrep*, a book published by LSAC itself, identifies the difficulty level of practice questions (Level 1 through 4, 1 being easiest), and explains the correctness/incorrectness of each of the answer choices to the questions. Studying these explanations by the test designers provide you critical insight to the tricks of the test.

You may find one-on-one tutorial assistance to be a valuable means of overcoming specific hurdles confronting you on the LSAT. A tutor will, ideally, tailor your preparation to the nuances of your unique learning style, and to specific areas of the LSAT that will give you the biggest headache.

In addition there are classroom preparatory courses that focus upon specific test-taking techniques for the LSAT. Others assist with the time barrier. For example, LSAT Proctor is an affordable effective resource that focuses on the deadly time limits of the LSAT sections.

Which of these resources or a combination of them that will work best for you may be a function of not only your individual test-taking skills as applied to the LSAT, but also your financial resources and time schedule.

35. Use of the LSAT Preparatory Books

Investing in an LSAT test prep book is a relatively modest expenditure and provides you a portable resource. It can be a place to begin in your assessment and preparation plan. The Bibliography of this book includes several books published about the LSAT. There are official guides which are those published by LSAC. One already mentioned is LSAC's *Official LSAT SuperPrep*. LSAC also offers a series of past-test guides, such as *Official LSAT Prep Tests: 10 Actual (LSAT Series)*, which, as the title indicates, provides ten actual LSAT exams given in previous years. Bonnie Gordon's *The Official LSAT Prep Test with Explanations* details the reasoning behind the correct answers to the February 2007 LSAT.

There are also several excellent "unofficial" LSAT guides, such as Nova's *Master the LSAT*. This book offers a user-friendly approach to explaining the logic behind the LSAT with detailed explanations of solutions to the questions, and a companion software CD.

Another especially good book is The Princeton Review's *Cracking the LSAT* (2008 Edition), which provides a comprehensive approach to test preparation and each test section's subject matter, including two complete practice tests. Barron's also publishes LSAT prep books. Help sources that are classroom-based, like Kaplan, provide text materials included with their programs.

Do not grab the first book you see on the shelf and assume, or hope, that it will be the "bible" to get you the score you need for your choice of law schools. First take a free practice test and honestly analyze what you need. Then you will be able to survey the books on the market (online, in the library, at the bookstore) with an experienced eye and choose the one that speaks to you. Whichever books and resources you select, make sure they are the latest edition and up-to-date with the current LSAT style and format. LSAC is the final word on what to expect on the LSAT.

3

Designing a Holistic Preparation Plan

36. Map Your Preparation Plan

Preparing for the LSAT or any such endeavor is not unlike getting ready to run a marathon. In a sense, you are preparing for the first Olympic Trials of law school. Dedicate yourself to a schedule of preparation of at least several weeks, if not months, ahead of your LSAT test date. Within that preparation period, set aside a specific time schedule in blocks of time — daily/weekly/monthly — that you will dedicate to LSAT preparation. Most people live busy lives that require juggling to make time for that one more thing. You must make the LSAT preparation time one of your priorities. Schedule it like a required class or a second job, including all components that are suggested below that you include as a part of an overall holistic approach to preparation.

37. Apply a Holistic Approach to Preparing for the LSAT

Using the practice tests is an important component of your preparation plan, but there is much more to it. If, for example, you are stymied by Arguments or Games, plan for extra time to focus on that type of question and how the problem-solving process works for solving it quickly. Also, it is important to take care of your own mental and physical welfare as you prepare; in other words, take a holistic approach to preparing for the LSAT.

38. Discover and Utilize Your Cognitive Style

Academic performance has long been linked to learning style, which is how an individual processes information. Each person has his or her own learning style; knowing yours should provide you insight for choosing your preparatory resources. Richard Felder and Barbara Solomon of North Carolina State University have developed and provided a free online assessment tool — just answer 44 questions and receive an immediate report of your learning style.

Professor Felder's assessment tool recognizes the various ways people learn which he describes as a combination of: active or reflective, sensing or intuitive, visual or verbal, sequential or global. Most people learn through a composite of these styles with individual variances. What do these styles mean?

39. Are You an Active or Reflective Learner?

An active learner does best in a learn-by-doing approach. This is the person who never bothers to read the assembly instructions. Even if he reads the instructions, the active learner will not understand them well until he actually dives into the components and does it. The reflective learner, on the other hand, prefers to study the instructions first before touching anything for assembly. The active learner will hop on the horse and learn to ride by falling off a few times. The reflective learner will want to read about riding the horse and have an instructor demonstrate riding the horse.

Both styles have their attributes. In the LSAT context, the reflective learner may have the advantage of more easily reading through weighty texts for the questions, but on the downside, may be slower to reach a result than the LSAT time constraints allow. As will be seen in discussing each of these learning styles, the key is to try to develop the best of both styles; to be adaptable to different situations.

40. Are You a Sensing or Intuitive Learner?

As Bruce Torf and Robert Sternberg point out in their book, *Understanding and Teaching the Intuitive Mind: Student and Teacher Learning*, people who are strong, intuitive learners arrive at a conclusion without consciously thinking about how they worked it out. To a certain extent, they automatically relate new concepts to prior knowledge and preconceived notions.

Intuitive learners are more comfortable with abstract principles and conceptualizing relationships between ideas.

Professor Felder notes that sensing learners on the other hand "remember and understand information best if they can see how it connects to the real world." Sensing learners are comfortable with many facts and details, and do better with concrete examples than intuitive learners.

Applying these learning styles in the LSAT world, if you are a sensing learner, you may have more trouble with the time limits of the LSAT sections. If you are primarily intuitive, you may be less panicked by the concept of time limits, but may have a tendency to be impatient, and miss a detail that is the key to the correct answer.

41. Are You a Visual or a Verbal Learner?

As the name implies, visual learners acquire knowledge and retain it best through what they see. Pictures, graphs, charts, diagrams, and visual demonstrations are all examples of important aids for the visual learner; a visual learner will prefer a picture or a diagram to assemble an item. A verbal learner will need to read the assembly steps written out in text. A verbal learner is primarily an auditory learner and will be more comfortable than a visual learner when dealing with material imparted through lectures and texts. Although both visual and verbal learners' styles will benefit from using notes and diagrams on the LSAT to assist in decoding the questions quickly, their use will be especially critical for the visual learner.

42. Are You a Sequential or a Global Learner?

Sequential learners acquire information best in a step-by-step format, each new concept relating to previously acquired knowledge. Global learners, on the other hand, are "big picture" people. In the forest and tree analogy, global learners need to first define the parameters of the forest. Sequential learners are happy to form or discover the forest one tree at a time.

Considering that humans are cognitively complex beings, we each have our own combination of these learning styles. Certain types of learning styles will be more natural to you than others. Yet if you learn more easily through one approach as opposed to another, you should recognize what you need to do to compensate for how that style may impede or assist you in a timed test situation. For example, a strong intuitive and global learner has a natural tendency to miss details. In the realm of test-taking, the intuitive learner inherently has a better chance of missing a key point in a question, leading either to a wrong answer or too much time spent on the question. Details will be particularly important both in the Analytical Reasoning and Reading Comprehension sections of the LSAT. If you do not assimilate details naturally or quickly, the need to do so will slow you down unless you have studied and improved this aspect of your style during your LSAT preparation.

If you identify and understand your particular learning style or combination of styles, and how those styles affect your own unique method of processing information, you will be able to pay attention to things you would otherwise miss. This is especially valuable information in your LSAT preparation because you can practice for the test armed with this knowledge, and improve your speed in comprehension and problem-solving techniques. Consider your learning style in choosing the preparation aids you will use in your plan. If you find yourself stymied and do not understand why a question type is difficult, a skilled tutor can help you further analyze your personal learning style and show you how to use it to your advantage on the LSAT.

43. Hone Your Critical Thinking Skills

An oft-repeated phrase in the context of law school admissions, and LSAT skills is "critical thinking." You have already read this term several times in this book. What, exactly, is critical thinking?

In its detailed exploration of the subject, The Foundation for Critical Thinking summarizes critical thinking as "universal intellectual values that transcend subject-matter divisions: clarity, accuracy, precision, consistency, relevance, sound evidence, good reasons, depth, breadth, and fairness." It is a cognitive, integrative function that embodies the ability to bring objectivity and acute observation into the process of synthesizing facts, drawing logical inferences, and reaching rational conclusions.

Critical thinking is not a static black-and-white process. It requires imagination, ingenuity, and empathy. It calls upon your ability to see another's point of view, and also to recognize the strengths and shortcomings of your own point of view. Simply stated, critical thinking is a highly integrative mental process. Its purpose and function integrate to understand viewpoints, test arguments, and solve problems.

Central to critical thinking is the understanding of assumptions and how they work. Poor assumptions lead to bad decisions, while well-grounded assumptions lead to success, growth and productivity. Many questions on the LSAT deal with conclusions based on assumptions, challenging the test-taker's insight and recognition of whether they are flawed, sound, missing, or incomplete. Critical thinking is seamlessly entwined with command of language, which is why vocabulary is such an important component of assessing one's ability in critical thinking.

According to James J. Messina, Ph.D. and Constance M. Messina, Ph.D., **www.coping.org**, the brain's highest cognitive processes that comprise the skills of critical thinking are interpretation, analysis, evaluation, inference, explanation, and self-regulation. Each of these elements has a place in the LSAT's question structure.

Interpretation

Using interpretive ability, people comprehend and express meaning or significance in a lifetime of experiences, situations, data, reading, judgments, beliefs, rules, procedures, literature, and language. Interpretive skills are most often invoked in the Reading Comprehension and Logical Reasoning/Argument sections of the LSAT; these questions call upon you to be able to decode, clarify and classify meaning. You are using interpretive skills when you identify the author's theme, purpose, or point of view in a passage. You are using interpretive skills by recognizing words that paraphrase an idea in different words.

Analysis

Through the employment of analytical skills, Dr. Peter A. Facione of Insight Assessment explains that people seek to "identify the intended and actual inferential relationships among statements, questions, concepts, descriptions, or other forms of representation intended to express belief, judgment, experiences, reasons, information, or opinions." In the Analytical Reasoning/Games section of the LSAT, the test challenges the ability to understand and sort out relationships according to specific facts and descriptions of how they work and the limitations on their function.

In the Logical Reasoning/Argument and Reading Comprehension sections, analysis is used in conjunction with the skills of interpretation and evaluation. In the process of analysis, you will be called upon to identify and examine ideas, analyze arguments, and recognize and understand — and possibly challenge — assumptions, or recognize and factor in missing assumptions.

Evaluation

With the skill of evaluation, Dr. Facione explains that you assess the credibility of a person's statements or descriptions of his "perception, experience, judgment, belief, or opinion; and to assess the logical strength of the actual or intended inferential relationships among statements, descriptions, questions or other forms of representation." Evaluation may include making judgments about the credibility of an argument based on the strength of its logical underpinnings. This skill also is precisely involved in the LSAT's Reading Comprehension and Logical Reasoning/Argument sections. Do the premises given support the conclusions? Is there a missing assumption?

Inference

Much is said about inference in critical thinking especially in the practice of law. The concept of circumstantial evidence rests on inference. No one was present when the tree fell in the forest, therefore, no one could hear if it made a sound, but you infer that it made a crashing noise when it hit the ground. You did not see Jane shoot her husband, but you find her standing over him with a gun in her hand. Ballistics and skin evidence show the gun is the one that killed him, and that she fired it. You infer she fired the fatal shot.

To make a credible inference requires identification of information that will ground a reasonable conclusion and predict consequences. Inference is inherent in legal reasoning, and is involved in many LSAT questions either by requiring you to recognize an inference and its fallibility, or to make an inference yourself based on the information presented in the passage and the question.

Explanation

As Dr. Facione continues to describe, explanation in critical thinking is "being able to present in a cogent and coherent way the results of one's reasoning. This means to be able to give someone a full look at the big picture: both to state and to justify that reasoning in terms of the evidential, conceptual, methodological, criteriological, and contextual considerations upon which one's results were based; and to present one's reasoning in the form of cogent arguments." Explanation is how the results of reason are conveyed to justify a conclusion in terms of evidence, method, and procedure. It is part of the persuasive stage of argument and is involved in various ways in the LSAT's Logical Reasoning/Argument sections in particular. In the Logical

Reasoning/Argument section of the LSAT, for example, you may be called upon to identify an explanation for how a conclusion is reached from a set of facts or a description in a passage.

Self-regulation

This is perhaps the overriding consideration within the critical thinking process, because through it, a person sifts through the other processes of critical thinking to test the validity of his own judgments. Are the conclusions reached justified by sound reasoning, or are they born of bias and sloppy inferences? Some people would call this form of self-monitoring "integrity."

Understanding the role of critical thinking in the LSAT test world will help you orient yourself to approaching the questions and understanding the expectations of the test questions. The LSAT is about working within – and staying within — a mindset.

44. Select Where You Will Prepare

In the early days of your preparation, you may benefit from the cloistered approach. Choose locations for preparation time that will not be prone to interruption by people, calls, noise, and other personal distracters that may make competing demands on your time and concentration. This could be a quiet corner of a library, a private study room, or office. One person arranged to use a neighbor's basement office to escape his own hectic household. Another rented a room at a budget motel.

As you begin to seriously pace yourself in simulated test conditions, you should add to your selection of test venues those public places that have environmental conditions with distracters that are similar to the real test situation, such as people sitting nearby tapping their feet, coughing, and rustling paper.

It may not be practical for you, or you simply may not have the time to move around to different venues for your test preparation. A practice aid offered by Virtual LSAT Proctor, can be extremely helpful in simulating the test environment and practicing the test within the LSAT sections' rigid time limits. Virtual LSAT Proctor produces an affordable DVD designed to simulate the conditions as you practice the test, being mindful of LSAC's prohibition of digital timers.

45. Turn Off Your Mobile Phone and Avoid Other Distractors

Effective test preparation requires dedication and focus. You need to know what and/or who your distracters are — those who would interrupt you. Place yourself where those distracters are not located, and cannot find you. You are not allowed to have your mobile phone while taking the LSAT. Why have it at hand while you are preparing for the test?

46. Concentrate on Solving Problem Areas

If there is a type of question on the LSAT that is particularly troubling — get help — then set aside specific times to work on it alone. If it is assumptions, for example, seek out those specific types of questions in the practice guides, and study how they work. Talk to a tutor. It is not uncommon for one or two types of questions to be a person's blind spot on a test like the LSAT. In dealing with this particular hurdle, consider and remember the following:

1. Put it in perspective. If it is a specific type of Games question for example, do not overspend your time on it to the exclusion of other questions you need to practice; for the simple reason that (a), Games is one of four graded sections; and (b), that one type of Games question is only part of the Games section. It does not impact your score, relatively speaking, as Logical Reasoning/Argument questions do.

2. Get help with the question style. It is more efficient to allow someone to help you who understands it, and knows how to teach it.

3. Work it out by diagramming its structure. All question types lend themselves to diagramming their structure — not just the Games.

4. Do not obsess about the problem. Practice it, set it aside, and work on the rest of the LSAT questions, coming back to the problem later.

5. Do NOT keep doing more of the same type of question hoping that repetition will turn on the light. That approach might work but it is unlikely. And it will take more time than you have or need to put to it.

If time management is your problem, do not panic early in the game. If you find you are consistently too slow for the LSAT's restrictions, any or all of the following could be happening.

1. You are easily distracted. If this is the case, you must work out a system for yourself that blocks out what is going on around you while you are focused on the LSAT questions. The meditation and hypnosis techniques suggested in this book may be valuable tools for attention problems. Do you have Attention Deficit Disorder (ADD)? It is not uncommon in exceedingly bright people for this malady to manifest itself with the onset of young adulthood. It is something that must be diagnosed and treated by a physician. It cannot be assumed to be an existing problem, nor should it be discounted as nonsense. If you believe you have the symptoms of this disorder, it would be worth consulting a physician who understands the problem; either rule it out or obtain proper treatment.

2. You are a slow reader. Most of the LSAT experts do not recommend "speed reading" courses per se. The reason they do not is that classic speed reading utilizes a scanning technique that, by definition, excludes words on a page. Because the LSAT passages are so densely constructed, − chocked full of significant words − the classic speed reading approach can be dangerous leading to missed key words and concepts. If you are a slow reader because you are a person who silently and laboriously "reads aloud", a basic speed reading lesson or two may help you break out of that pattern. Some people who have made it through undergraduate school reasonably well are slow readers because of this pattern. For some reason, this reading mode does not manifest itself or is less of a hindrance in computer interaction, but the LSAT is a paper and pencil test, not an interactive computer test.

If speed reading is not an option that appeals to you or seems inappropriate in your case, consider consulting with a reading specialist if you find that regular LSAT timed-test practice does not improve your speed on the Reading Comprehension and Logical Reasoning/Argument sections after your first weeks of practice.

3. You are not doing sufficient practice under real-time simulated test conditions. Use simulated timed test conditions with proctor assistance, such as Virtual LSAT Proctor.

4. You are doing too much of your practice on the computer instead of the paper and pencil practice with an answer sheet that simulates what the real Test Day will require.

5. You are allowing yourself to become hung up on specific problem areas that are sidetracking you from moving on through the test in a paced regimen.

6. Test anxiety is getting in your way. There are several things you can do to overcome this which are covered in this book.

7. Consider getting your eyes checked. An amazing number of people overlook something this simple in their day-to-day lives. If you need reading glasses or a prescription change in the glasses you wear already, now is the time to find out and remedy it.

8. Where and when are you practicing? You may be using an unsuitable location, one prone to interruptions and distractions.

9. Did you devise a preparation plan? Are you following it?

10. Are you turning off your mobile phone, pager, and e-mail while working on the LSAT materials?

47. Prepare Yourself Physically

Why is your physical condition relevant to preparation for a test that evaluates your knowledge and mental capacity while you sit in a chair pushing a pencil? This is an experience that takes a physical toll on everyone. At a minimum, and under stressful conditions, you need to physically sit still, and remain acutely alert for a full half-day with only one short break. If you are physically too tired, ill, or incapacitated on "test day," you would do better to cancel the test and reschedule. Whatever your overall physical health is on a day-to-day basis, you will want to maximize it positively for the LSAT.

Your LSAT preparation map, therefore, should include time to enhance your physical well-being; your plan should include regular physical exercise. This approach may include such activities as: walking, jogging, dancing, running, swimming, horseback riding, golfing, tennis, racquetball, biking, stationary cycling, skating, cross country skiing, weight training, stairmaster, jazzercize, team sports, or gym training. Let the LSAT be the reason to do whatever you like, or can most easily force yourself to do, and benefit from it. Your choice of exercise should include cardiovascular or aerobic exercise which increases the heart rate for 20 to 30 minutes. Examples of aerobic exercise are fast walking, jogging, running, swimming, cycling, racquetball, skating, and cross-country skiing.

In the context of LSAT preparation, two key proven health benefits of cardiovascular exercise are improved stamina and good mental health. These activities benefit heart function, which in turn improves the delivery of oxygen to your brain; as a result, you will think better. This is not an unproven, hypothetical devise to market fitness products; although it helps them. With an aging population of baby boomers in the United States coupled with high profile individuals with Alzheimer's like President Ronald Reagan, concerted research has been encouraged regarding the effects of aging in high cognitive brain function; what it is, exactly; and what happens to the areas of the brain controlling memory, thought, quick thinking, complex problem solving, and logic.

While all the biological answers are not yet identified, there is an undisputed linkage between high stability of these brain functions and cardiovascular fitness. Studies report that the human brain may begin to lose some of its adaptability as early as the third decade of aging, but can be offset by the benefits of physical exercise. The common factors are the delivery of oxygen to the brain, and the number and strength of the connections between brain cells. These are extremely powerful indicators of the link between physical activity and learning. One significant study that confirms the importance of this principle has been done by the University of Illinois, published in 2004. This study concluded that aerobically trained, physically fit individuals demonstrated better performance in the cognitive functions of memory, attention, and processing of information for correct problem solving.

For a lot of good health reasons and to enhance your prospects for good test performance, exercise should be mapped into your

LSAT preparation plan; at least 20 to 30 minutes of cardiovascular activity three times a week, while being mindful of any restrictions or modifications your physician may place on such a program. This plan will, on a regular basis, exercise your muscles, increase your heart rate and blood flow, and on the whole, improve your physical stamina. Most importantly, your brain will work better in preparation for the LSAT marathon. Do approach your physical preparatory work within the limits of reason. Now is not the time to risk injury with something new or too difficult; tailor your workouts to your ability and overall physical shape, and work up from there.

A good measure of whether you are overdoing it is whether you can talk while exercising; exercise experts refer to this as the "talk test." If you are exercising, and breathing comfortably, you will be slightly breathless but still able to carry on a conversation during your exercise. If you cannot talk because you are too winded to speak, then you are overdoing it, and need to slow down. If you are not winded at all — you can speak too easily — you should intensify your workout.

If you are not used to exercising regularly start slowly. Simply getting out for a walk in the fresh air is a good starting place. Anything you do will have a multi-beneficial return: (1) cardiovascular benefits, and (2), a relaxing mental break from other activities and stressors.

If you are already into a regular exercise routine, the worst thing you can do is abandon it for more time sitting in a chair going over LSAT materials. Stay with your routine, and evaluate how you might use it to optimize your LSAT preparatory plan.

Not all exercise needs be cardiovascular, although the portion of your program dedicated to aerobic activities will benefit you. Several types of exercises can be done while sitting on a chair. For easing the strain of long-seated work, there are isometrics: alternately tightening and relaxing the leg, shoulder and gluteus muscles, stretching, and quiet, deep breathing exercises. The advantage of seated isometric exercises is that they are not difficult to insert into your daily routine. Their use can be as simple as doing them while seated at your desk or watching TV.

If you do not usually exercise, or if you plan to add something new to your program as part of your preparation plan, you should consult your physician before trying anything strenuous.

48. Eat Right — Eat Well

While it should go without saying, nutrition is an important factor in preparing for the marathon LSAT. Many people characteristically abandon good eating habits to catch every minute possible in comprehensive study routines. As suggested by the now-coined phrase "you are what you eat," the link between good diet and good performance is not a new idea. It is a simple equation: food intake affects body chemistry, including chemicals in the brain, which in turn affect how you feel and how you think.

People often do not carry this universal principle into helpful practice; either because it is too easy to catch fast food on the fly or because they do not truly understand, or believe in, which food selections are likely to enhance their mental acuity. "Brain food" means lean protein, carbohydrates, and fats consumed in balanced meals — not feast then famine — and certainly not empty calories. "Fat" has become a dirty word in the American craze to be thin and cholesterol-free, but not all fats are bad. The brain itself is more than 60 percent fat. It is covered by a myelin sheath that is 75 percent fat. Fats also play the role of messengers in the brain. The Omega-3 fatty acids are critical dietary components for effective brain function.

In *The Brain Diet*, Harvard lecturer Alan C. Logan, ND, FRSH, convincingly explains and discusses the connection between diet and mental health, and intelligence. Dr. Logan stresses the importance of Omega-3 supplements (fish oils being a key ingredient, found in foods like wild salmon), purple/deep red fruits such as blueberries, green foods containing magnesium, the spices turmeric and ginger, and green tea. Other studies support these foods as boosters for brain power. Also recommended are avocados — said to be as powerful as blueberries — nuts, seeds, and dark chocolate. If you are a finicky eater and cannot overcome your distastes, or have allergies to certain beneficial food sources, investigate supplements that will provide these optimal diet ingredients.

Vitamins and minerals are also important components — especially the B complex. Further studies have shown that vitamins A, C and E, which are antioxidants, have contributed to maintaining memory in the elderly; it follows that these dietary components may enhance memory for all of us. The minerals calcium, potassium and sodium are also reported to be important to maintain energy balance and good brain transmitter functions.

49. Drink Plenty of Water

What you drink is also vital. Studies have revealed that most people are partially dehydrated most of the time. If the brain is dehydrated, it simply will not function as well; it is a simple cause and effect. The best drink to enhance intense mental work is pure water. The adage of at least eight glasses of water a day continues to be true.

50. Do Not Permit Test Anxiety to Sabotage You

While studying for a test a certain amount of concern can be motivational, but panic or high anxiety will interfere significantly with your effectiveness and can sabotage all your efforts on Test Day. Anxiety is a behavioral, psychological, and physical reaction all at once; in reality, test anxiety is a form of self-sabotage. It is akin to actor's stage fright where the mind goes blank when the curtain goes up. Such anxiety can be so severe that it causes physical symptoms including chest pain, dizziness, hyperventilation, insomnia, sweating, and nausea.

If you have had trouble with tests in the past due to such stage fright, or if you have experienced any level of anxiety that interferes with your focus, memory, concentration or similar skills, you must confront it head on. If you have experienced test anxiety before, you will find no panacea in the LSAT without assistance. People have dealt with this issue successfully in a number of ways. Central to overcoming the problem is: (1) focusing on effective studying, (2) utilizing a holistic approach to your preparation, (3) knowing — and believing — that you are well prepared, and (4) keeping the importance of the test in perspective. When all is said and done, it is still just one test. Despite intellectually understanding this truth, conscious logic and reason alone rarely cure high anxiety. Specific techniques are available to overcome this problem.

51. Counseling Helps Dispel Anxiety

Most people, exceedingly normal people, live in denial of the need to actively deal with test-taking or any form of anxiety. One source for overcoming test anxiety is professional counseling. A counselor can assist you in confronting your problem, recognizing the source of your anxiety, and identifying effective coping skills. Unreasonable anxiety is often brought on and exacerbated by certain triggers, and you may not realize what these triggers are. Discovering them through professional assistance can help you neutralize them. If you suffer physical manifestations of anxiety you should consult with your doctor to work in concert with your counselor.

52. Meditation, Retreats, and Prayer Can Improve Test Scores

Meditation and Yoga

Meditation techniques are proven methods of successfully coping with anxiety. Meditation is the act of calmly focusing on a single pleasant thing, such as a sound, an image, a mental visualization, or the simple act of breathing. Meditation can be engaged in groups and individually.

One well-known meditative approach is yoga. Yoga is a centuries-old discipline. It is believed that the practice of yoga originated in India; the term yoga refers to union or communication, or joining body and mind through spiritual and physical discipline. The core techniques of yoga are controlled breathing and posture. Yoga practitioners claim that yoga positively affects cognitive functions, specifically attention span and memory. Improved memory and concentration, without question, are two key skills for test taking and studying, making yoga an attractive companion to study technique.

The ultimate goal of yoga is to reach complete peacefulness of body and mind, helping you relax and manage stress and anxiety. Traditional yoga philosophy teaches that its adherents should develop yoga techniques through behavior, diet and meditation. If you simply are looking for better stress management for your LSAT preparation and not an entire lifestyle change, yoga can still help. Yoga has many styles, forms and intensities; but Hatha Yoga, in particular, may be a good choice for stress management. This style of yoga is designed to encourage a calmer mind, along with improved physical flexibility.

There are several versions of Hatha Yoga. Which version you choose depends on your personal preferences. All varieties of Hatha Yoga include two basic components: physical poses and breathing. Proponents emphasize that coordination of mind, body, and breathing through Hatha Yoga can improve physical, psychological, and spiritual well-being.

You do not need to be an athlete or even particularly flexible to practice Hatha Yoga; it is considered suitable for people of all abilities. In a typical Hatha Yoga class, you may learn anywhere from 10 to 30 poses. Poses range from the easy pose of lying on the floor while completely relaxed, to the most difficult poses that take years of practice to accomplish. Those poses which help you relax, focus, and de-stress are the poses to consider for LSAT preparation.

Regardless of which type of yoga you choose to practice, you have the freedom to choose the poses most comfortable and relaxing for you. Controlling your breathing is an important part of yoga because yoga philosophy views breathing as the core of your vital energy. Yoga teaches that controlling your breathing can help you control your body and gain control of your mind — reining in thoughts that may distract you from achieving a goal, interfere with studying, or induce stress and anxiety. Through yoga, you learn to control your breathing by the simple act of noticing it, offering a good tool for stress management and relaxation. Left unchecked, stress and anxiety cause many types of physical ailments, and sabotage academic endeavors.

To combat a complexity of physical and mental self-sabotage, the practice of yoga involves a series of physical poses accompanied by mind-clearing meditation. Many of these simple yoga exercises work in concert with meditative techniques to clear and calm the mind. The benefit is a sense of well-being, confidence, and renewed energy. These attributes can only enhance a person's ability to study for an experience like the LSAT.

The emphasis of a specific yoga approach, be it mental or physical well-being, will depend on the orientation of the teacher. The beauty of yoga as a method of improved mental techniques that will translate to higher test scores is in the variety of approaches it offers. Yoga classes, tapes and videos are readily available for learning and practicing yoga techniques. Your favorite bookstore and public library are handy resources. The following are some online starting points:

- **http://www.yoyoga.com/tapes.html**

- **http://www.yoga-for-health-and-fitness.com/books/yoga-book-store.htm**

Meditation and Retreats

Jay A. Cutts, a professional educator who develops individual tutorials for several national graduate exams, including the LSAT, has spent about 30 years in personal meditative work. He endorses meditation and regularly participates in silent retreats: **http://www.swcp.com/jcutts/meditation/retreat.htm#DecidingToGo** About the notion of retreat, Mr. Cutts advises:

"Retreat is a unique opportunity to enter into silent presence, supported by the energy of others doing the same, much more deeply than can usually be done during our regular life schedules. This kind of work, boosted by group dialogue and one on one inquiry, can directly clarify our deepest life concerns and transform strongly ingrained habits, releasing long held anxieties and allowing our energy to flow more freely. It can allow the possibility of coming freshly and intimately in touch with life itself, perhaps in a complete fresh way."

Mr. Cutts also cautions that you should take care in selecting a retreat. Be sure you understand what the program will entail and determine if it resonates with what you need or hope to achieve.

Scheduling a retreat within your LSAT preparation plan may be a powerful aid for boosting your ability to concentrate, focus, and combat test anxiety. In this regard, carefully explore retreat locations and programs. Not all will be your cup of tea or helpful or even affordable, but there are many options available around the country, and also around the world, from half-days up to a week or more. How might a retreat fit into your LSAT preparatory plan? Consider weaving a retreat into a place on your preparatory schedule where it is most likely to provide you the rejuvenation you need and be the most beneficial to you. For some people, this may be at the beginning, before even starting actual LSAT preparation. Others may find it well-timed to schedule a retreat at the end of the preparation as a bridge from preparation to Test Day. Yet another permutation could be a time-out within the preparation plan to take a rest and allow what has been studied to settle and resonate before returning to the final stage of preparation.

There is no one perfect formula. The point of these suggestions is that you should consider what fits your unique style and needs, and your schedule. What you should not do is reject the notion as impossible, silly, or a waste of time. Just as your physical being needs sustenance, your mind needs just as much if not more.

Some online sources of retreat information are as follows:

- **www.retreatsonline.com** — This site advertises some 2,000 retreat options worldwide, encompassing many different focuses, including yoga and meditation retreats ranging from a day to a week and more at various locations around the country and around the world.

- **www.dharma.org/ims/** — Located in Barre, Massachusetts, the Insight Meditation Society's emphasis is on meditation and spiritual renewal through two options: retreats organized at its Retreat Center or at its Forest Refuge.

- **www.sacredtravel.org/** — This retreat program is centered at beautiful Assisi, Italy, focusing on contemplation, meditation, and silent retreats for spiritual renewal.

These are just some noteworthy sources. Religious-based programs, and nondenominational and secular-based retreat options can be found everywhere. A suggested approach to using retreats in the context of LSAT preparation would be to incorporate a retreat at the beginning of your preparation program and/or near the end of it not long before Test Day. Your purpose is to de-stress, and remove yourself from anxiety. Even if it is just a partial day retreat it can be a powerful mind aid and reducer of test anxiety.

Qigong

Similar in some respects to yoga, but perhaps more actively physical by comparison, is the Chinese technique of Qigong (pronounced chee gung), which combines breathing exercises with relatively easy physical movements. A form of Qigong, perhaps more commonly known is Tai Chi, or Taiji Quan, is a practice much like dance but in smooth, gently controlled slow motion.

Qigong has been practiced in China for thousands of years, and recently has been studied for its effectiveness in relieving chronic illness and the stress of anxiety with favorable results; so much so that it is being studied by the National Institutes of Health. The Qigong Research & Practice Center, online at **www. Qigonghealing.com**, explains Qigong as "the art and science of using breathing techniques, gentle movement, and meditation to cleanse, strengthen, and circulate the life energy." The Qigong exercises consist of a series of slow regulated circular exercises accompanied by regulated breathing, and focused posture. It can include self-massage and manipulation of pressure points similar to acupressure. It is an acquired art, but in a simple beginning mode it can be self-started.

In Chinese, qi means energy, your life force, and gong means skill or practice. More than just physical movement, Qigong is designed to be practiced by anyone. Some of the exercises can be done simply standing or seated. Qigong exercises have been reported to improve immunity to disease, lessening of pain, relaxation, and -- especially applicable to studying for tests and banishing test anxiety -- improved attention span and mental tranquility.

Best known for its medical benefits, Qigong also has gained a following in the business world. Lawyer and international negotiator, Julian Gresser, endorses Qigong for promoting a "sense of connectedness, coherence, wholeness, and vitality" but most especially integrity, "the capacity of every living thing to hold its own in the face of entropy, disorder, and uncertainty, its ability to carry on its life, however, humble." A directory of Qigong teachers and therapists by state is currently available at **http://www.Qigonginstitute.org/listing/directory.php**.

Prayer

Akin to meditation is the power of prayer, a meditative-type practice that is at the center of most religious beliefs. Prayer is an intensely personal, and profound experience which benefits those who embrace it. Like yoga and other meditative practices, prayer can be engaged in both individual and group practice.

The power of prayer has been the subject of scientific study. For example, studies have validated the power of prayer in healing.

One doctor, as a first-hand observer, reports that the patients who pray are "happier, seem to have less depression and seem to cope with life's challenges, including health challenges." The role of prayer should not be discounted or overlooked in combating anxiety and improving your confidence. Physicians who understand this do not regard prayer as an occasional phenomenon or eccentricity of patients, but rather as an integral factor in patient care, recognition that human beings are comprised of body, mind and spirit. Many surgeons begin a medical procedure with prayer with their patient. This holistic view of well-being translates to maximizing a person's potential in all areas of their life.

The common thread in all these approaches is the banishment of paralyzing negative energy through a disciplined mind centering, to generate and enforce a positive outlook within. Controlled slowed breathing, mind-centering, and relaxation are important elements of the process — a letting go of negative thoughts which are self-destructive and mentally distracting — and with them, letting go of your test anxiety.

53. Use of Breathing Exercises for Pacing and Relaxation

In *The Art of Breathing*, Nancy Zi recognizes the central role of controlled breathing in meditation and reduction of anxiety. Calling the practice Chi yi, Zi notes:

"The demands of today's society, working conditions, and environment are complicated and frequently stressful; and our energy needs, both physical and mental, are forced to change rapidly to cope with all the forms of tension to which we are subjected. Innumerable varieties of relaxation techniques – transcendental meditation, self-hypnosis, physical exercise, biofeedback, and many others – are available today. But no matter what method is practiced, a mode of breathing in one way or another always comes into the picture."

Zi explains that Chi Yi is breathing to the core, centered within four to five inches below the naval. It is a visualization concept of deep breathing beyond just filling the lungs with air. It is more about centering, balance, storing of energy in a calming way. This seemingly simplistic revelation resonates particularly well for students preparing for college entrance exams, clinicals, medical boards, and bar exams. It carries through not only the preparation phase but also into the examination environment of Test Day.

A Five Minute Breathing Exercise

The following statements describe a simple breathing exercise.

1. Sit upright in a comfortable, relaxed position, in a quiet place, eyes closed.

2. Place your right hand on your abdomen at approximately your navel position.

3. Place your left hand lightly on top of your right hand.

4. Exhale.

5. Breathe in deeply on the count of 5.

6. As you breathe in, think of nothing but the feeling of breathing; you should feel your body push out against your hands as you in inhale.

7. Hold for the count of 3.

8. Exhale on the count of 5. Your hands will relax inward with your body. Feel your whole body relax. Sense a floating feeling.

9. Repeat several times thinking only of the feeling of breathing in and out slowly and peacefully, relaxing further with each breath intake and exhale.

54. Therapeutic Massage for Stress Relief

A more passive but nonetheless therapeutic relaxation technique is massotherapy. There are several versions of therapeutic massage which promote relaxation, and the release of anxiety. These can range from deep tissue to light touch techniques. Some involve applications of hot stones or towels, Reiki, and acupressure. If prescribed by a physician, massage may be covered by some health insurance plans, so you should check this option before assuming you have no coverage.

55. Acupuncture to Reduce Anxiety

Acupuncture is another ancient, Asian, alternative medical practice that has gained increasing favor in Western culture for treatment of many types of maladies, including stress and anxiety-related problems. In terms of Chinese medicine, acupuncture interrupts the flow of energy that allows stress to build — sort of an escalation like a race car, and giving it an off ramp. In terms of our Western culture's medical interpretation, acupuncture when properly practiced releases endorphins in the brain which induce a feeling of relaxed well being, allowing the need to react to stressors to step down and take a break. The result is a relaxed state that allows you to return to task in a state of well being, in which you are better able to function, and be more open to receiving and learning new information.

56. Hypnosis as a Tool for Improving Test Scores

Hypnosis is a surprisingly common source of help at the university level to improve study skills and test performance; this is not the nightclub trick of turning volunteers into chickens. Hypnosis is a state of relaxation induced by a skilled hypnotist, in which the mind is highly focused while in a relaxed state, and open to cues and suggestions; in this regard, it shares with meditative strategies the attributes of relaxation and focus. Kevin Linehan of OnTrac Hypnosis and Wellness Center of Atkinson, New Hampshire, explains that hypnosis helps students and test-takers by "addressing stress, memory recall, confidence, study habits, motivation and classroom attention. Every person will have one or more specific issues that if improved would dramatically affect grades and test scores in a positive way."

As early as 1954 a Stanford study found that post-hypnotic suggestion with hypnotizable students improved their schoolwork. Another example of the effectiveness of hypnosis was reported in 1993 by Harry Stanton. In this study, a group of 11 medical practitioners who had failed their fellowship exams received two 50-minute sessions of hypnotherapy for improving confidence and overcoming their test anxiety; 10 of the 11, thereafter, passed their tests.

Hypnosis, obviously, is not a resource for amateurs. Skilled professionals, on the other hand, can help many people. The ultimate tool is learning how to practice the art of self-hypnosis which can be learned and developed through professional guidance.

Your hypnotist, counselor, instructor, and spiritual advisor cannot accompany you on LSAT Test Day, but they can assist you in making the most of your preparation plan and diffusing the debilitating interference of text anxiety.

57. Biofeedback to Control or Reduce Test Anxiety

The Mayo Clinic endorses biofeedback as a method of improving health. Scientific studies have established that biofeedback can assist people in training their minds and bodies to overcome many problems, including migraine headaches, depression, high blood pressure, and notably, for purposes of LSAT preparation, anxiety. Biofeedback is an ability acquired through working with a specialist who uses signals from special monitoring equipment of physical signals to teach a person how to control body functions, and mental responses.

The biofeedback therapist may use several different techniques to gather information about your body's responses. Determining the one that's right for you will depend on your particular health problems and objectives. Biofeedback machines and techniques include:

Electromyogram (EMG). An EMG uses electrodes or other types of sensors connected between you and a machine that detects the level of muscle tension, and alerts you to increased tenseness so that you can learn to recognize the feeling early on and associating it with the tension you want to decrease before it becomes a problem. EMG is mainly used to promote the relaxation of those muscles involved with backaches, headaches, neck pain, and teeth grinding (bruxism) — all which are well-established companions of anxiety. It follows that if you can control these physical manifestations of anxiety, you will benefit mentally as well. An EMG also may be used to treat some illnesses in which the symptoms tend to worsen under stress, such as asthma and ulcers. The machine's sensors assist in physically training you to overcome anxiety before it gets underway; it is a self-imposed physical intervention to a problem that has mentally inhibiting factors as well.

Temperature biofeedback. In this approach of biofeedback, sensors attached to your fingers or feet measure your skin temperature. Because your extremities' temperature often drops when you are under stress, a low temperature reading of these areas can prompt you to begin relaxation techniques, and prevent the onset of a problem. This technique has proved particularly useful for migraine sufferers, an affliction of concern for test-takers. Other anxiety induced problems may be forewarned and avoided by learning how to increase the temperature in the body's extremities.

Galvanic skin response training. In this version of biofeedback, sweat is presumed to be an indicator of stress. Sensors attached to your skin measure the activity of your sweat glands and the amount of perspiration on your skin. This information can be useful in treating emotional disorders such as phobias and anxiety attacks. If you suffer from severe test anxiety, as diagnosed by a doctor or therapist, you may want to explore this type of therapy as an option for treatment. Note that any of these biofeedback interventions are interposed through exploration with medical providers who have first provided medical input as to whether their use has a likelihood of success. Not all levels of test anxiety demand biofeedback as a treatment. Nevertheless, phobic or severe and regular anxiety responses may benefit from these procedures.

Electroencephalogram (EEG). An EEG monitors the activity of brain waves linked to different mental states, such as wakefulness, relaxation, calmness, and light and deep sleep. EEG may be used to diagnose and assist in the treatment of a variety of conditions, including insomnia, epilepsy, and other neurological disorders. People with chronic anxiety may manifest several related physical symptoms. The mind-body connection is complicated. An EEG is not necessarily a component of, or prerequisite procedure to, the use of biofeedback. Depending on a person's presentation of symptoms, a physician may consider an EEG to rule out problems as much as to diagnose them.

Some of these procedures may sound severe and far out in the context of preparing for a law school entrance exam. Nonetheless, if test anxiety has plagued you in the past, and threatens to derail you on a chosen career path that you believe is otherwise right for you, then you may well be right to pursue such diagnostic options. Information can be just as useful in ruling out what is not a problem as it is in identifying one. Following a holistic approach to readying yourself for the LSAT, or any other major test or endeavor, means being proactive in recognizing ways to overcome both physical and mental obstacles.

58. Attune Your Study Time to Your Own Rhythm

Any classroom teacher knows, and many studies have confirmed, that efficient learning and retention of concepts normally drop dramatically after about 45 minutes. This will vary somewhat among individuals and environmental factors, but the point is the same; spend too long at something, and you reach a point of diminishing return. Do not perseverate on one type of study beyond your mental fatigue factor, especially in the early days of your LSAT preparation. The LSAT requires a half-day of focus but in 35-minute increments. You will need to be able to shift easily from one type of concept to the next; use this fact to your advantage in your preparatory sessions. Plan your preparation schedule according to your individual learning style as much as possible. If you are a "morning person," you are not going to do well studying at midnight; if you are a "night owl," the midnight hour may be the optimal time for you.

59. Avoid Fatigue with Rest and Breaks

The fact that fatigue affects attention span, and ability to learn is so well-known as to be axiomatic. Yet effective rest is one of the least-used tools by students preparing for exams. In the push to accomplish a task on a deadline, effective sleep is often the first to go. Sleep deprivation negatively and significantly affects the brain's attention span, and retention of information.

Especially when you are working on difficult problem areas for you on the LSAT, give yourself a chance to absorb and process the practice test and explanations; then give yourself a break. It also is difficult for the brain to assimilate new concepts when stressed by fatigue. Your preparation plan should include time for rest and relaxation. Your exercise and meditation, or equivalent program, fits in here.

60. Commit Your Preparation Plan to Writing

It may be fine to scope out in your mind how you intend to prepare for the LSAT, but the best approach is to lay it out on a calendar — a written schedule of time, place, and activities. The length of time, place or places you choose, and components of your preparatory program will be directed by your unique personal strengths and weaknesses; discovered in your initial self-assessment. If you are using multiple help sources, map out how and when you are fitting them into your practice schedule. Divide your blocks of time into segments of the LSAT subject areas— Games, Arguments, Reading Comprehension — scaled in time for where your needs lie.

61. Develop a Realistic Schedule

Although you may find that you need to adjust it as you go along, your written plan gives you a template against which you can check your progress in developing your confidence and growth in understanding of the LSAT. It also will put your plan into the perspective of small blocks of time, instead of looking at a huge mountain of time looming before you; with the LSAT perched at a peak out of reach. Use a calendar to block out your time — and dedicate your time — for your work on the LSAT preparation.

62. Select Practice Aids Suitable for You

There are a large number of preparatory aids on the market. These by and large break down into classroom courses, preparatory books, online courses, online practice aids, interactive exercises, and private tutors. Your own schedule demands and learning style will determine which of these are best for you. There are resources available to assist in your assessment. An individualized tutorial resource may be helpful in resolving your unique strengths and weaknesses. You can recognize for yourself that you score low on the Games questions, but you may not be able to determine why you are scoring low on certain types of problems.

Some people are sufficiently self-disciplined to map a preparation with a self-study approach using a prep book, practice tests, and online resources. Others who are procrastinators or just do better with more structure, and discussion with others, will do better with an interactive or structured approach, such as a tutor or classroom program can provide. The classroom courses, such as Kaplan's, capture you in a structured schedule dedicated to the LSAT. If you are not a person who self-starts easily or if you tend to procrastinate, the structured classroom courses or personal tutor may be a good investment for you.

63. Take Time to Survey the Available Resources

There are many good practice aids on the market. If your budget limits your choices, survey the costs of prep-test books and online resources. These are likely to be less expensive than the full classroom courses and personal tutors. Since the approaches of these practice aids differ, you should not seize the first one you find. Take a little time to fully survey the market's offerings, and choose what makes sense for you and your budget. On the other hand, do not be tempted to overly scrimp, as you are at the threshold of a lifetime profession. Preparing for the LSAT is an investment in your future.

64. Include Real LSAT Tests in Your Practice

You can order past real LSATs from LSAC. Your plan should include time to go through the preparatory material you have chosen, taking practice LSATs under simulated test conditions, breaking the test down into the various types of questions, learning and practicing test-taking techniques, and making time for yourself to de-stress with healthy options such as exercise, meditation, right diet, recreation, and rest. The key is to devise a program on a consistent schedule designed to help you improve your score on the LSAT.

65. Plan for no Surprises on the LSAT

Preparing for the LSAT is analogous to preparing for a marathon, and you want to "peak" at the right time. Many LSAT prep materials suggest starting six months in advance of the date you will sit for the exam, while others recommend two to four months as sufficient; some people may not have the luxury of sustained study over six months.

For purposes of providing an example, the following outlines a hypothetical eight-week preparation program. If you have selected an optimal six-month plan, the final two months could be similar to the following, but with fewer practice tests per week. Whatever your schedule is, you should organize and map out the days and weeks on a calendar. The following simply summarizes one example of a two-month preparatory map. In deciding how you will set up blocks of prep time within this schedule, consider spaced time periods rather than a mass-attack approach. Studies indicate that students perform better on tests when they have used smaller increments of study spaced with breaks for other mental and physical activities. The cram-for-the-exam approach is far less effective, especially for tests like the LSAT.

Week 1 — Take a mock LSAT from start to finish, observing the time restrictions for each section to get a feel for the test. Analyze your results from score to problem areas, and your reaction to it, among other things. Take a break, and work several sample or "mini" tests. Survey practice aids and programs. Map out your preparation program, including time(s) and place(s) where you will study for the LSAT. Acquire practice aids. Sign up with programs and/or tutors if you have selected these aids. Order real past LSATs from LSAC. Begin meditation or other mind-centering exercises at least 5 to 15 minutes daily. Structure aerobic exercises — 20 minutes each Tuesday, Thursday, Sunday; one-mile walk each Monday, Wednesday, and Friday; Saturday, day off except for meditation or other mind-centering exercises.

Week 2 — Simulated practice test; full LSAT from LSAC taken within the time limits under simulated test conditions, using a proctor aid. Follow your selected practice aid program, having mapped it for completion over the next seven weeks, plus work with practice aids specifically for logical reasoning. If you are a slower reader than the LSAT demands, investigate increased speed reading techniques for reading comprehension and test-taking. Maintain physical exercise program and mind-centering exercise of Week 1; meditation/ mind-centering exercises 10 to 15 minutes daily — even in as little as five-minute increments.

Week 3 — Start the week with a new simulated practice test; assess score and types of problem questions. Consider if your selected preparatory program is addressing the areas where you most need help, and adjust if necessary. Follow your selected practice aid program, plus extra time with practice aids for your specific problem areas. Play logic games daily and continue your physical and mental exercise schedule.

Week 4 — Work on specific types of questions you find most challenging for your LSAT practice tests. Continue physical/mental exercise regimen and your selected practice aid program. At the end of the week, self-assess your comfort level with each area of LSAT to determine your focus over the next four weeks. If you are utilizing a single weekend course aid, you might include it at this point in your preparation schedule. Take a full practice LSAT under proctored simulated conditions at the end of the week end. Saturday: day off.

Week 5 — Continue focused work on areas of the LSAT. Assess the amount of time you have spent the previous four weeks on each type of LSAT section. Have you ignored or spent relatively too-little time on any type of question? Midweek: take a full LSAT test you have not reviewed before under simulated test conditions. Compare your score to earlier practice tests. Continue your selected practice aid program, focusing on areas revealed in the latest practice test analysis, working with practice aids for problem areas. Continue your physical/mental exercise schedule. If you are feeling increased anxiety at this point, expand your physical/ mental exercises. If you feel that you are reaching a block, consider consulting a tutor or mentor.

Week 6 – Follow a lighter schedule this week. Play games. Continue your selected practice aid program. Follow your physical/mental exercise schedule. Relax.

Week 7 – Cover the preparatory material for the Writing Sample section of the LSAT, and practice outline and writing. Continue your selected practice aid program; work with practice aids for any continuing problem areas to boost your comfort level. Observe your physical/ mental health regimen. Take an additional day off from preparatory work, preferably mid-week. Focus on Arguments and Reading Comprehension practicing under simulated proctored conditions in real time.

Week 8 — Inventory your checklist for Test Day; where it is, the time required to get there, where to park when you do get there, know how long it will take you to get from the parking to the test room; is it paid parking? What to take and not take with you; if possible, visit the room or at least the building where the test will be held; your entry ticket; what you will wear — cold room, warm room, layers if you do not know?. Make sure you plan for a good night's sleep the night before. If it will help your morale, take a final practice full LSAT under simulated conditions early in the week — not on the day or night before Test Day. Observe your physical/mental health routine.

66. Stick to Your Program

Having gone to the trouble of mapping out and embarking on LSAT preparation, an important key to your success is going to be your ability to follow your map. It is easy to allow other priorities of life to erode your schedule, steal time from your study periods, and distract you. Some changes and adjustments are inevitable, especially if you have overreached your capability to follow your study plan. In this case you will need to make adjustments that comport with reality. Such adjustments are not the same as procrastinating. The point is to lay out a program to give yourself a map, or schedule, that accounts for all the components you need to cover for best preparation in the time you have.

4

General Test Taking Techniques

The LSAT is a multiple-choice test. There are several test-taking techniques applicable to multiple-choice questions. There are universal techniques that serve well on most tests and some that are particularly important in polishing your LSAT acumen.

67. Preview/Orient Yourself to the Test Section Before Starting the Questions

When the proctor says, "Begin," take a few seconds to initially scan the test to settle your thinking for the subject matter of the section: logic, reasoning, or reading comprehension. Shut out those around you. You do not want to know what they are doing or how they are reacting. You cannot afford to be distracted, and it is likely that several around you will have a different version of the test; or even a different section of the test than you have in the same time period.

68. Read the Directions

Each section of the LSAT starts with a brief statement of directions; please read them. Some test prep experts advise that if you are well-prepared in advance, you can skip the directions and save time. This seems to be a bit risky for a couple of reasons. First, the LSAT in front of you on Test Day is unique. It may differ in any number of ways from the practice tests you saw in your preparation. Second, the test directions introduce the type of questions, and tell you the approach expected. For example, often the directions will mention that "more than one choice will appear to be a possible answer." This is a clue to which type of quirky questions will follow.

Also, the directions will cue you to the subject matter of the section. For the Logical Reasoning/Argument section, the directions will mention that you are to analyze or evaluate the reasoning presented in textual passages and answer the questions accordingly.

The Analytical Reasoning/Games section will be introduced with directions stating that you will be presented with groups of questions based on specific sets of conditions, and may suggest that you create diagrams to assist you in answering them.

The Reading Comprehension section directions will tell you that passages will be followed by questions about what they state or imply; often with more than one correct answer; from which you are to choose the best answer. The Reading Comprehension section often differs from the Logical Reasoning little more than its passages are longer.

Do not assume, therefore, that you can skip these directions to save time because you have done so much preparation. The directions can actually assist you, and save you time in the long run because they give you the opportunity to orient your mind for the section.

69. Tune into LSAT Vocabulary

Some deceptively simple words have their own meaning in LSAT-speak. Often words that we use casually in everyday speech can become potential land mines in the context of an LSAT test question; one example is the word "most." In everyday vernacular, "most" is used to convey the concept of "many" or a "majority," It generally is not a word used to convey the concept of "all." On the other hand, the word "most" may have a more specific application when it appears in conclusions or answers on the LSAT. Normally, the definition of "most" on the LSAT means a majority that does not rule out the concept of "all."

In Logical Reasoning and Reading Comprehension problems, be aware of words that will alert you to shifts in concepts or drawing of comparisons. These are words and phrases such as "on the other hand," "still," "nevertheless," "along the same line," "moreover," "in contrast," and "similarly." These and words like them signal that the writer is setting up a juxtaposition of ideas or points. They may be premise and counter-premise statements. Such transition words tell you whether the writer thinks the concepts are alike, e.g., "similarly, " "moreover," "along the same line," or contrastingly different, counter-premise, or qualified in some way, e.g., "still," "nevertheless," "in contrast," "on the other hand." As long as you are alert to these words, they can actually help you decipher what is going on.

70. Answer the Easy Questions First — But Stay in Order

Do you remember the 1.4 minutes per question rule? The easy questions will take you far less time than that. The LSAT questions are not ordered by level of difficulty. The most difficult question in the section could be the first or last question, or any question in between. Move through the test and bypass those questions that threaten you. Mark those on your answer sheet and return to them. This will optimize your chance of recording the correct answers to the questions that are the easiest for you, which increases the likelihood of a greater number of correct answers and fewer guesses. Be careful in scoring your answer bubbles so that you do not get your answers out of order on the answer grid. Keep your answers in order.

71. Be Methodical and Consistent

Do not rush yourself. The LSAT psychology is to entice you to rush, and through rushing, sabotage your concentration so you forget everything you learned in your preparation. You have prepared for the test and practiced it within the test's schedule; stick to your plan. The LSAT sections are designed not to be completed by most people. Rushing to get through them can result in more wrong answers than working through them at the pace you developed in your practice tests. You will have taken many practice tests and developed a strategy for working through each section in its time limits. One strategy is to identify the easy questions first, nail those, and keep moving on through the test to the harder ones.

72. Read the Question Asked Before the Proposed Answers

There may be red herrings in both the textual passages of the questions, and in the proposed answers. Some answers will be keyed to points relevant to the material, but they will be answers to different questions than the one you are asked to answer. Understanding the question asked before reading the answers will make the red herrings less enticing; first read the questions asked.

73. Read all the Proposed Answers to the Question

A typical feature of the LSAT multiple-choice questions is that there is often more than one seemingly correct answer, requiring you to chose the "best" right answer. There will often be an obviously incorrect answer that you can immediately eliminate. Reading all the answers before selecting the best answer avoids missing the "best" answer, and also may assist in quickly eliminating the clearly wrong answers.

74. The Best Answer often has the Most Information

Especially where more than one answer seems to be correct, look at which one has the most information. If it is a correct statement, and answers the question, it will most often be the best answer. The other "correct" answers, by comparison, will likely be more generalized; less specific to the question asked.

75. Be Attentive to Grammatical Consistencies and Inconsistencies in the Question Structure

Which of seemingly equal correct answers is most symmetrical with the grammatical structure of the question or the statement to which it relates in the passage? An example best illustrates this concept. In a passage the writer states:

"Women in the workplace still have to fight to break through the glass ceiling. Despite great strides made since the advancement of the harassment laws and Equal Pay Act, the insidiousness of discrimination has not gone away, it has simply gone underground."

Question: Which of the following is the best statement about the author's view of gender discrimination in the workplace?

(A) The Equal Pay Act has improved working conditions.

(B) Discrimination creates a glass ceiling in the workplace.

(C) Despite the laws protecting women from discrimination, it continues in the workplace.

(D) The discrimination laws do not work.

(E) Women can break the glass ceiling.

The easiest answer to discard is (A). The next easiest one is (E). They both may be true, as nothing in the passage directly contradicts them, but neither is on point to the theme of the passage. (D) is next discarded because the author's reference to "great strides" counters the premise that the laws do not work. That leaves (B) and (C), both consistent with the author's premise, are they not? Which do you pick? (C) is the most closely a restatement of the author's words, and ties in the continuance of discrimination "despite" the protection of the laws. (B) refers only to the glass ceiling which the laws were intended to remove. In this question, (C) is the best answer, and its structure, beginning with the word "despite" is the clue.

76. Be Alert to Negatives and Double-Negatives

The use of negatives paired in sentences such as, "not," "no," "neither," "nor," "nobody," and "nowhere," is nonstandard English and can be conceptually confusing. Our normal use of language does not often employ double negatives, since they are easy to misread; an example is, "He hardly had none." Two negatives cancel each other out. Therefore, this sentence means, "He had some" or, "He had at least one." In the vernacular though, the speaker might mean, "He did not have any." See the confusion? On the LSAT, a double negative is an alert to be careful and do not fall into the vernacular usage. Consider the literal meaning.

77. Your First Answer is Often the Right Answer — But...

Assuming you have not misread the question the common rule is: your first answer is the best one. Although in *Tips for Multiple Choice Tests*, Professor Scott Plous of Wesleyan University, while acknowledging the legitimacy of the "first answer rule," advises that, "you shouldn't be afraid to change your original answer if, upon reflection, it seems wrong to you." According to Professor Plous, studies conducted over 70 years have proved that "students who change dubious answers usually improve their test scores" more than half the time. The key is not second guessing yourself when you have applied your best effort, but rather in recognizing those questions which you misread, where you missed a critical point, or in which you simply failed to notice the correct answer.

Professor Plous' advice may leave you wondering how to know the difference. The key is catching what is a clear error of judgment in reading a question. That is something entirely different than following your instinct in choosing between two seemingly correct, or close, answers to a question you have studied. In the latter case the "first answer rule" is the one the experts recommend you follow.

78. Answer all the Questions

An unanswered question on the LSAT is a guaranteed wrong answer. There is no benefit in leaving a question blank on the LSAT because there is no penalty for a wrong answer; even a random guess is better than no answer at all. There are a few tricks of test-taking that can reduce "random" to "better odds" for selecting the right answer.

79. Employ the Educated Guess

Many questions will contain answers that you will quickly recognize to be incorrect. Eliminating answers improves your odds of selecting the correct answer from the remaining options.

In the time allowed for each question, the educated guess at one of two possible answers may be the best you can do. You can mark it, and return to it if you have time, but do not shy from selecting your educated guess. According to the "first answer rule" mentioned above, if you have correctly read the question, your educated first guess on the two possible answers is likely to be the correct one.

80. Use Diagrams and Notes to Aid You in Working Out an Answer

Although you cannot bring any notebooks or even blank paper into the test with you, you are permitted to use the blank spaces in the test booklet to make notes, lists, and diagrams. In reading through the text of a question do not hesitate to highlight or circle key words, make notes in the margin, and mark questions you are skipping; just to name a few tips. For the Analytical Reasoning questions in particular you will find that sketching diagrams can be incredibly helpful.

81. Avoid Answers with Absolutes

Certain words can be keys for eliminating answer choices. Answers that contain words such as "never," "all," "every," "none," "always," "absolute," or "always," are more often than not the wrong answers.

82. Be Alert to Faulty Logic Traps

Be alert for the "if-then" traps that often appear on the LSAT, in either the Arguments or Games sections. These can appear as faulty assumptions. A simple example is:

- A group of men and women is playing croquet together on the lawn.

- All of the men are wearing white shirts.

- Therefore, all of the people on the lawn wearing white shirts are men.

The problem with this conclusion is that it makes a leap from what the men are wearing to what all the women are wearing as well. There is no premise for what the women are wearing. What is the missing premise to make the conclusion true? None of the women are wearing white. The faulty logic is that if the men are wearing white, the women must not be wearing white. The two are not mutually exclusive unless you are given a premise that expressly states so. This example also illustrates that dangerous word "all" in LSAT-speak, and also the missing premise situation.

83. If Running Out of Time — Use the Same Letter for all Remaining Questions

If you are nearing the last two minutes of an LSAT multiple choice section and find panic rising as you realize there are five questions you have not yet read. Despite all your planning and preparation, this section — possibly the Experimental one — has derailed your momentum. You will not have time for educated guesses on these questions; the LSAT proctors relentlessly enforce the time restrictions. If you are caught with unanswered questions when time is called, you will not have the chance to fill them in. If you leave them blank, of course, you are guaranteed five wrong answers.

Statistically, the order of the correct answers will vary on multiple-choice tests so that one particular choice position is not over-weighted. Nevertheless there are only a finite number of answers per question. Any one letter, therefore, is statistically going to be repeated over a group of questions. If you randomly fill in the answer bubbles for those last five questions, the odds are overwhelmingly against your guessing any of the correct answers. Choose one letter such as "B" — or any letter that feels lucky — and quickly fill in that same bubble for each of those five blank questions before time is called. The odds are much better that at least one, if not more, of those five questions will have a "B" answer; or whichever "lucky letter" you have chosen.

5

Practice, Analyze, Practice

A key component of your preparation plan is devising ways to hone your skills. You can, and should, do more than just take and retake the practice tests. Since none of those exact questions are likely to be repeated on the LSAT version you will take for real, you should familiarize yourself with techniques that help you select the right answers. Because the mind's learning process responds best to variety, you are well-advised to rotate and expand practice techniques in your preparation plan.

84. Build Your Vocabulary Skills

Robert J. Sternberg of Yale University, writing as a contributor in, *The Nature of Vocabulary Acquisition*, affirms that vocabulary "is highly predictive, if not determinative, of one's level of reading comprehension," and "the best single indicator of a person's overall level of intelligence."

There are various strategies for enhancing your vocabulary. The least effective is trying to memorize lists of new words and their meanings. Putting words to use in speech or writing will associate them with words and concepts already familiar to you. Another method of expanding vocabulary is wide and varied reading. The more you expose yourself to new words in context, the faster you will assimilate new words. Two indispensable tools at your elbow while you are reading are a thesaurus and a dictionary; either in hardback or electronic forms, or both. Use a dictionary that will emphasize current meanings, such as the Merriam-Webster New Collegiate Dictionary.

Use the dictionary in tandem with your LSAT practice tests. If you find a weakness in word knowledge, which is slowing down your reading rate or obscuring your ability to correctly interpret LSAT passages or questions, look them up. Do not be satisfied with just passing by a word's meaning. Look up synonyms, antonyms and various other forms of the word as well. Questions will not be repeated on LSATs, but vocabulary may be.

The LSAT does not present specific vocabulary questions, but the Reading Comprehension and Logical Reasoning/Arguments sections in particular demand a broad and sophisticated command of language. The following words and phrases illustrate the level of vocabulary you are likely to encounter in LSAT passages or questions. They are provided here to give you a feeling for LSAT vocabulary level.

- Empirically verifiable
- Phytoplankton

- Zooplankton
- Intrinsically evaluative

- Protagonist
- Esoteric

- Subsidiary conclusion
- Celestial

- Unambiguous
- Cultural chauvinism
- Intrinsically
- Prodigious
- Polemical
- Veracity
- Obtuse
- Effloresce
- Disingenuous
- Renege
- Turbulent
- Orthodoxy
- Globalization
- Ergonomic
- Paleontology
- Histology
- Ambiguity
- Supersede

- Eurocentric
- Indigenous
- Hegemony
- Paradigm
- Misanthrope
- Laconic
- Canon
- Fallacy
- Precursor
- Xenophobia
- Metaphysical
- Obliterate
- Paradox
- Darwinian
- Profiteering
- Climatology
- Precedence
- Angst

- Ambivalence
- Exegesis

- Predisposition
- Harmonize

- Consistent
- Photophobia

- Anaerobic
- Morbidity

- Lucidity
- Omniscience

- Prescience
- Concupiscence

Lighthouse Review's, *The Ultimate Verbal and Vocabulary Builder for the SAT, ACT, GRE, GMAT, and LSAT* is a useful tool to include in your cache of LSAT preparatory materials. This vocabulary building book utilizes a workbook format of vocabulary building exercises and vocabulary quizzes. It is a user-friendly and handy resource for an extra boost in your LSAT preparation. You can tuck it into a briefcase or backpack for reference in those odd moments such as waiting for appointments or simply a mental escape from the usual intensity of LSAT preparation. Nova's companion CD to *Master the LSAT* also covers vocabulary building including a work session on word analysis; the art of deducing a word's meaning from its parts.

Word analysis is one way to penetrate an unknown word, but because the primary acquisition of vocabulary is accomplished inherently by deducing a word's meaning through context, the LSAT will test not only your vocabulary knowledge by throwing in esoteric words in passages and questions, but also your ability to derive meaning from context. There often will be a signal to the meaning in the question's structure that makes the difference in decoding a question.

The correct answer in Reading Comprehension questions frequently will be a close paraphrase of a statement in the author's text. If you do not know the meaning of the key words in each statement — the author's or the answer's — you may not recognize the correct answer; or, the strangeness of a key word may derail you if you are not paying attention to the language structure in the answers. Consider the following hypothetical example that is similar to the type of question you might encounter in a Reading Comprehension section on the LSAT.

In the Reading Comprehension passage, the writer states that "this artist's sgraffito should be viewed only after drinking a bottle of cheap Chianti."

A question that follows asks: Which of the following best expresses the writer's opinion of the artist's work?

(A) The artist should stick to sculpture.

(B) The artist is a master at oil painting.

(C) The artist is not very good at plaster decoration.

(D) The artist works best when drunk.

(E) The artist should drink Chianti before working.

First, what is the tenor of the writer's opinion of the artist's work — good or bad? Even if you do not know that Chianti is wine, the phrase "cheap bottle," coupled with the need to drink it before viewing the artist's work, suggests something is needed to fortify one before looking at the artwork, and that the artwork is not deserving of anything pricey; all of which implies through use of sarcasm a negative criticism of the artwork. The implication that one needs to be inebriated on a cheap wine even more strongly indicates a negative opinion.

The drift of the writer's negative statement quickly rules out (B), because (B) is a complimentary statement. (D) and (E) also can be ruled out because in the passage the writer is referring to the viewer needing to drink, not the artist. This leaves you to consider (A) and (C), which are not so immediately distinguishable from each other because they both appear to be derogatory conclusions about the artist's work, which is "sgraffito."

At this point the meaning of the word "sgraffito" is the key to whether the best answer is (A) or (C). If you do not know what sgraffito means, you might take an educated guess; that sgraffito is a fancy word either meaning, or related to, the word "graffiti," a word referring to obscene doodling by vandals on city walls and subway trains; therefore, being used by the writer here as a derogatory metaphor for the artist's painting or drawing. With this interpretation, you would likely rule out (C) because it refers to something that is not painting or drawing, and by process of elimination, choose (A) as the best answer because it at least implies the artist should not be painting or drawing.

You would be wrong.

"Sgraffito" is a method of making ornamental plaster surfaces by scratching designs into the plaster to reveal the paint color underneath. (C) is the correct paraphrase of the author's negative opinion of the artist's sgraffito. Quickly knowing the meaning of the word leads you to the correct answer without having to analyze the other answers in the way described above.

You could get this answer right, even if you do not know the meaning of sgraffito, by paying attention to the form in which the answer choices are stated. If you have never heard of "sgraffito," instead of being seduced by the similarity of the word to the word graffiti — which is not used or referenced in any of the answers — look at how the answers are constructed. Only two are phrased in a way that could be a paraphrase; for example, the definition of sgraffito. (B) says oil painting and (C) says plaster decoration. The question asks for a correct statement of the writer's opinion. If it is a good opinion, the answer is (B). If it is a bad opinion, the answer is (C). You have interpreted the opinion to be negative because the writer states one should be mentally dulled by cheap wine in order to tolerate the artist's work. The correct answer is (C).

Vocabulary is language. The above example demonstrates there is more to good vocabulary skills than knowing the meaning of words, although the latter is certainly an important advantage.

85. Understand the Art of Analogy

A complex step forward from vocabulary study is understanding the use of analogy. Analogy, in its simplest form, is a comparison. An example of an analogy is the following:

Feline is to cat as canine is to: (a) bird (b) dog (c) cat (d) claw.

To select the answer, you must determine from the choice of answers the one word that relates to canine in the same way that cat relates to feline. First, of course, you need to know the meaning of the words. Then you have to be able to recognize the relationship between the words "feline" and "cat." Next, you must understand the relationship, or conceptual likeness, between "feline" and "canine." And finally, you must recognize the concept from the choices given, that relates to "canine" in the same way that "cat" relates to "feline." A cat is a type, a subset, of feline. Of the word choices given, "dog" is the type, or subset, of canine that completes the second pair for the analogy.

The cat/dog analogy is simple, but relationships, categories, and vocabulary governing analogies can be quite obscure and require not only word knowledge but mastery of recognizing relationships between concepts.

Although analogies per se do not appear on the LSAT, the mental process required to understand, recognize, and apply analogies is inherent in the LSAT; indeed, in the practice of law. The art of analogy is a significant process in solving problems, understanding concepts, making decisions, perceiving likes and differences, and explaining conclusions. Playing with analogies will not only provide vocabulary-building work but, even more importantly, develop critical thinking skills.

The role of analogy in legal reasoning is explained by Harvard professor, Lloyd L. Weinreb, in *Legal Reason: The Use of Analogy in Legal Argument*. Professor Weinreb posits that analogical reasoning is at the heart of our legal structure. It is how legal principles are propagated through case precedent. As discussed earlier in explaining the concept of *stare decisis*, when a court considers a case before it, the judge will often turn to how other courts have addressed similar issues or interpreted the law that governs a case. The lawyers will argue to the court how precedents apply, or alternatively, should be disregarded in this particular case. Analogy is inherent in this process, because without use of analogy, Professor Weinreb advises; a court's opinion would be incomplete.

If analogy is an important mental process in legal reasoning, it follows that it plays a role in those intellectual skills that the LSAT seeks to measure as predictors of success in law school. Using analogies as practice games for the LSAT makes eminent sense. Like the vocabulary practice, playing with analogies provides a mental break from the rigors of the more traditional LSAT practice; analogy continues to develop the type of thought process that is at the heart of the skills the LSAT is designed to identify and measure. Working on analogies, especially at the more esoteric level, serves to expand your vocabulary, another tool that will be helpful on the LSAT. One comprehensive source of analogies for word-game practice is the *Kaplan MAT, 2007-2008 Edition: Miller Analogies Test.*

Analogies can be set up in a number of ways. A language-based analogy would be based on word roots such as: word is to afterword as thought is to −?− (answer being "afterthought"). A history analogy would be: Washington is to Yorktown as Grant is to −?− (Appomattox). In a causal analogy, the first word is the cause of the second word − the effect. For example: water is to wet as freezing is to −?−(ice). The cat/dog analogy above is a type of categorical analogy.

A mental construct of the concept of analogy is the recently added feature of two passages to the Reading Comprehension section of the LSAT. While it is not so clearly set forth analogically as the feline/cat/canine/dog example, the thought process is not dissimilar. This type of Reading Comprehension problem involves reading and comparing two passages and answering questions about just one passage at a time. In a similar way, you compare concepts in determining matches and differences in analogy pairings. Consider the following hypothetical Reading Comprehension problem consisting of two passages and five questions. In LSAT time you would have seven minutes for this set.

Passage Number 1

Let us now briefly consider the steps by which domestic races have been produced, either from one or from several allied species. Some effect may be attributed to the direct and definite action of the external conditions of life, and some to habit; but he would be a bold man who would account by such agencies for the differences between a dray and race-horse, a greyhound and bloodhound, a carrier and tumbler pigeon. One of the most remarkable features in our domesticated races is that we see in them adaptation, not indeed to the animal's or plant's own good, but to man's use or fancy. Some variations useful to him have probably arisen suddenly, or by one step; many botanists, for instance, believe that the fuller's teasel, with its hooks, which can not be rivaled by any mechanical contrivance, is only a variety of the wild Dipsacus; and this amount of change may have suddenly arisen in a seedling. So it has probably been with the turnspit dog; and this is known to have been the case with the ancon sheep. But when we compare the dray-horse and race-horse, the dromedary and camel, the various breeds of sheep fitted either for cultivated land or mountain pasture, with the wool of one breed good for one purpose, and that of another breed for another purpose; when we compare the many breeds of dogs, each good for man in different ways; when we compare the game-cock, so pertinacious in battle, with other breeds so little quarrelsome, with "everlasting layers" which never desire to sit, and with the bantam so small and elegant; when we compare the host of agricultural, culinary, orchard, and flower-garden races of plants, most useful to man at different seasons and for different purposes, or so beautiful in his eyes, we must, I think, look further than to mere variability. We can not suppose that all the breeds were suddenly produced as perfect and as useful as we now see them; indeed, in many cases, we know that this has not been their history. The key is man's power of accumulative selection: nature gives successive variations; man adds them up in certain directions useful to him. In this sense he may be said to have made for himself useful breeds.

Passage Number 1

The great power of this principle of selection is not hypothetical. It is certain that several of our eminent breeders have, even within a single lifetime, modified to a large extent their breeds of cattle and sheep. In order fully to realize what they have done it is almost necessary to read several of the many treatises devoted to this subject, and to inspect the animals. Breeders habitually speak of an animal's organization as something plastic, which they can model almost as they please. If I had space I could quote numerous passages to this effect from highly competent authorities. Youatt, who was probably better acquainted with the works of agriculturalists than almost any other individual, and who was himself a very good judge of animals, speaks of the principle of selection as "that which enables the agriculturist, not only to modify the character of his flock, but to change it altogether. It is the magician's wand, by means of which he may summon into life whatever form and mould he pleases." Lord Somerville, speaking of what breeders have done for sheep, says: "It would seem as if they had chalked out upon a wall a form perfect in itself, and then had given it existence." In Saxony the importance of the principle of selection in regard to merino sheep is so fully recognized, that men follow it as a trade: the sheep are placed on a table and are studied, like a picture by a connoisseur; this is done three times at intervals of months, and the sheep are each time marked and classed, so that the very best may ultimately be selected for breeding.

Passage Number 2

The devil preaches evolution to call us away from the ways of God and into the iniquity of darkness and the future of our own destruction. The proof of what I say is grounded in the "Bible" which is the undisputed Word, the Truth, the Abiding Wisdom of God by which if we but listen, we shall be empowered to live a humble, fruitful, honorable life above the things that crawl, slither, walk on all fours or fly on the wing. He has given us humans dominion over these things as their keepers and stewards and to use them for our sustenance during our sojourn on this earthbound journey. It is blasphemy to preach that we humans possess the ability to change and create the beasts and fowl of the earth. This is proven in the "Book of Genesis," in which God tells us clearly, in verses 20 -30:

20 And God said, Let the waters bring forth abundantly the moving creature that hath life, and fowl that may fly above the earth in the open firmament of heaven.

21 And God created great whales, and every living creature that moveth, which the waters brought forth abundantly, after their kind, and every winged fowl after his kind: and God saw that it was good.

22 And God blessed them, saying, Be fruitful, and multiply, and fill the waters in the seas, and let fowl multiply in the earth.

Passage Number 2

23 And the evening and the morning were the fifth day.

24 And God said, Let the earth bring forth the living creature after his kind, cattle, and creeping thing, and beast of the earth after his kind: and it was so.

25 And God made the beast of the earth after his kind and cattle after their kind, and every thing that creepeth upon the earth after his kind: and God saw that it was good.

26 And God said, Let us make man in our image, after our likeness: and let them have dominion over the fish of the sea, and over the fowl of the air, and over the cattle,

27 So God created man in his own image, in the image of God created he him; male and female created he them.

28 And God blessed them, and God said unto them, Be fruitful, and multiply, and replenish the earth, and subdue it: and have dominion over the fish of the sea, and over the fowl of the air, and over every living thing that moveth upon the earth.

29 And God said, Behold, I have given you every herb bearing seed, which is upon the face of all the earth, and every tree, in the which is the fruit of a tree yielding seed; to you it shall be for meat.

30 And to every beast of the earth, and to every fowl of the air, and to every thing that creepeth upon the earth, wherein there is life, I have given every green herb for meat: and it was so.

Thus, the "Bible," God Himself, tells us that God has made "every living creature that moveth." The word, "every" means all of them, my brethren, not some of them. "God made the beast of the earth after its kind, and cattle after their kind, and every other thing. He made whales to swim in the seas, not some one-celled creature to be called a whale someday. He has given us "every herb bearing seed which is upon the face of all the earth and every tree." God has told us in Genesis that every single thing wherein there is life has been made by Him, not by us. We have these things for our use, our survival, our pleasure, if you will, of looking upon them or for their companionship. But let us not elevate and deceive ourselves that we are God. That belief is the ultimate sin that will lead us into eternal damnation.

Question No. 1: The best statement of the writer's main theme in Passage No. One is which of the following:

(A) Animals exist for the pleasure of humankind.

(B) Variations in domestic animal species are mainly attributed to man's selection by breeding for specific uses.

(C) Types of animals evolve according to their environments.

(D) Early humankind discovered wild animals that suited its purpose and tamed them for breeding.

(E) Sheep, horses, camels, dogs, and cattle are the best domestic breeds.

Question No. 2: The writer of Passage No. Two believes that human-directed evolution of domestic animals is:

(A) A sin

(B) Blasphemy

(C) Impossible

(D) Sacrilegious

(E) God's work

Question No. 3: Comparing the two Passages, one point where the two writers seem to agree is:

(A) A plant could change due to its habitat.

(B) God created heaven and earth.

(C) A Dipsacus is a remarkable machine.

(D) Humankind has dominion over animals.

(E) Animals are created perfect as we now see them.

Question No. 4: In Passage No. Two the writer quotes the *Book of Genesis* as his supporting evidence. What is the writer's supporting evidence in Passage No. One?

(A) Agricultural treatises

(B) Visual inspection of the changes caused by the animals' adaptations through human breeding choices

(C) Lord Somerville

(D) Youatt

(E) Judgings in Saxony

Question No. 5. Which of the following is the best argument for writer of Passage No. One to counter the reasoning of the writer of Passage No. Two?

(A) The *Bible* is not written by God.

(B) There are many animal species, like dinosaurs, not mentioned in the *Book of Genesis*.

(C) According to the *Book of Genesis*, God has given humankind dominion over all the creatures of the earth; therefore it follows that humankind holds within that dominion the God-given freedom to control how the animals are bred to each other to develop their various uses to serve man as God intended.

(D) Because animals have changed over time, we know they have to be different than they were at the time of the *Book of Genesis*.

(E) Several agricultural treatises have been written that show how breeding has changed and adapted various domestic breeds to provide better products or service for human use, thus proving that such change is a fact, not a hypothetical belief.

Commentary:

Question No. 1: The best answer is (B). This is one of the easier questions for this passage. The entire passage focuses on domestic animal variations being attributed to human breeder selection.

Question No. 2: This one is a bit trickier and requires you to read the question carefully. The question asks you for the writer's belief about human-directed evolution; that is, referring to the act of humans creating new and different creatures. The writer of Passage No. Two states that it is "blasphemy" to "preach" that humans can change animal species, and that only God can create. Therefore, the writer is saying that human directed creation is (C) impossible.

Question No. 3: This question poses that there is a point on which both writers can agree. If (D) is not readily visible as the correct answer, you can reach it by process of elimination. (A) is an evolutionary statement for which there is no evidence for agreement in Passage No. Two. Likewise, there is nothing stated in Passage No. One about the writer's belief about (B) God's creation. (C) is an incorrect reference to Dipsacus mentioned in Passage No. One, and Dipsacus is not mentioned in Passage No. 2; and (E) is the exact opposite of a statement made in Passage No. One. Both writers, each in his own way, refer to humans' dominion, or control, over animals, highlighting (D) as the best answer to this question.

In reviewing the possible answers to this question note a couple of things. There are at least two quick throwaway answers: (A) and (C). (B) comes close to being a throwaway as well, but is one that might give you a second's pause. You may be enticed to question whether the absence of any reference to belief by the writer of Passage No. One is enough to make an assumption that he would agree with at least an initial creation theory. (E) is another easily-dismissed answer if you read it correctly and realize it is the opposite of the writer's statement in Passage No. One; for example, "We can not suppose that all the breeds were suddenly produced as perfect and as useful as we now see them; indeed, in many cases, we know that this has not been their history." Therefore, the writer of Passage No. One would not agree with (E).

On the other hand, both writers, each in his own way, talk about humankind's dominion over all other life on earth. In Passage No. One, the writer talks about the many changes humans have made with controlled breeding of domestic animals. In Passage No. Two, the writer quotes repeatedly the *Bible's* use of the word "dominion" with regard to man's relationship to the creatures of the earth.

Question No. 4 follows the LSAT guideline that the answer with the most information tends to be the correct one when all of them seem to be correct. Here, the writer of Passage No. One cites all the items mentioned in the answers as evidence of his point, but what they all have in common is that their evidence arises from their observation of the animals that are the product of breeding decisions.

Question No. 5 presents a debate premise question. Which of the given answers best counters the argument presented in Passage No. Two? There are various ways to counter an argument: (1) prove a statement supporting it is false; (2) provide additional evidence that counters the argument's evidence and changes the conclusion; (3) point out a fallacy in the argument; (4) point out a missing premise in the argument; (5) illuminate a faulty or missing faulty assumption; (6) show another conclusion is possible from the same premise. One of the most successful ways to counterargue is to use the other person's own premise to your advantage; the latter is useful for this question. In Passage No. Two, the writer's premise is that evolution is not possible according to the *Book of Genesis* in the *Bible* because it says that God created all life on the earth. Also the writer acknowledges that *Genesis* reports that God gave humankind "dominion" over all the other creatures of the earth. Dominion is control. Choosing how to breed domestic animals is a form of control. Therefore, it can be argued that through humanity's "dominion," breeding selection is carrying out part of what God intended for humans to do with animals. The answer that represents this concept is (C).

What about the other answers? (A) is a theological statement that relates to what a person believes about the *Bible*. It is not related to the question of evolution. In the context of these passages, (B) and (D) are both similar in that neither relates to human-controlled evolution and therefore can be eliminated as not relevant evidence. Further, many animals are not specifically mentioned in *Genesis*, but they are all covered by the broad categories of walks, crawls, swims, and flies, among others. Agricultural treatises, mentioned in (E) do not work either because they extol human controlled evolution; the writer of Passage No. Two will simply dismiss them as blasphemy. They cannot be directly related to any statements in *Genesis*. As the writer of Passage No. One, your best approach to counter the conclusion of Passage No. Two is to show that your premise is consistent with writer No. Two's interpretation of *Genesis*. The best answer to this question, therefore, has to be (C).

86 . Practice Can Be Fun — Play Games

Many kinds of logic and analytical games are available to enhance your skills. The vocabulary exercises, puzzles and games can be played when you find yourself waiting for an appointment, on a break from work, or other activity. Some can be played on the computer; others with pencil and paper. Most are available at the library, some are free online, and others may be purchased at a minimal cost of the daily newspaper.

87. Play Sudoku

Virtually every newspaper, many magazines, the Internet, and puzzle books galore carry Sudoku puzzles. Sudoku is a logic game that does not require language or understanding of mathematics, although it uses the numbers 1 through 9. It consists of a game board composed of nine square grids, each grid containing nine blocks. When completed, the board will have nine rows horizontally and vertically each containing the numbers 1 through 9, and each nine-block grid will contain the numbers 1 through 9 within it. A few numbers are randomly revealed on the board to provide a starting point. Those revealed numbers cannot be changed. From that beginning, you have to deduce which numbers fill in the remaining blanks.

There are levels of difficulty, and also variations on the basic Sudoku premise. In addition to the daily newspapers, there are Sudoku puzzle books and online game sites: **www.websudoku. com** and **www.sudoku.com**. Practicing Sudoku "on the go" will help keep your "logic muscles" limber.

88. Online Logic Games

There are many online logic games to stretch your mind besides Sudoku. Some tricky, logic puzzles are available at **http://www. rinkworks.com/brainfood/**; the site provides Logi-Number Puzzles. These are interesting because they are similar to the principle of rules in the LSAT Analytical Reasoning/Games section. These puzzles combine numbers and logic, provide a puzzle grid, and lists rules that apply to completing the grid.

89. Analyze the LSAT Analytical Reasoning/Games Section

This section of the LSAT is like the awesome, fearsome Wizard of Oz; a fellow with a few slight of hand tricks up his sleeve standing behind a curtain. He is not a bad guy; if you draw back the curtain the intimidation disappears. The key to these questions is to demystify them with lots of practice, and let them be fun.

Analytical Reasoning is LSAT's puzzles and games, which is why playing all kinds of games for fun is a recommended past time; in addition to your serious prep time. These games will keep your brain limber. Although LSAC has yet to convince anyone that the Analytical Reasoning/Games section truly tests lawyer skills, it does test the ability to quickly work puzzles under pressure. This section generally consists of four Games covering 22 to 25 questions. Because each test edition is unique unto itself, this is an estimate based on past history of the test. As has been mentioned, drawing a diagram in your test booklet of the conditions presented for each Game will be immensely helpful.

If you do nothing else in your practice of the Games section of the LSAT, practice diagramming so that you are accustomed to quickly and methodically doing it in a way that makes sense to you.

All the experts and LSAT survivors unanimously agree — keep going on the Games section. Do not freeze on any one Game or question. The best advice on the proctor's "go" is to survey the section, and work first on the Game that you like to do best. Work through that one, bubble the answers to its set of questions, and choose the next one you like best.

When you set up a diagram, survey the rules and immediately plug in any definite givens; item or items that are immutable. In the football carpool example mentioned earlier, an immutable was that Jane had to drive her own car. Some of the rules will allow for variables but only for certain variables. LSAC is looking for you to conceive the setup spatially that is in three-dimensions. Since you cannot bring in little 3-D objects, the drawings are the next best way to represent the conditions.

Each Game has a list of people, objects, animals or items. Most of them will have some mobility according to rules about how they are related to each other and in what specific space; around a table or in some kind of collection or categories (grouping); in a lineup or on days of a week or month (ordering); or even combinations of groupings and orderings. There can be logic statements such as "If Jane is next to Joe, then Ann is next to Sue." Diagram the game layout and use it to apply the questions.

90. Analyze the Arguments Section of the LSAT

The Logical Reasoning/Arguments sections are 50 percent of the test, and it is important to commit a corresponding portion of your practice to the Argument type of question. In practicing the Argument questions you should pay close and careful attention to the words used. Deceptively simple words or phrases such as, "some but not all," "but," "however," and double negatives are deadly if overlooked or misunderstood in context.

Remember, the Arguments section of the LSAT is not about arguments in the sense of disputes and disagreements. They are about reasoning skills— finding flaws in reasoning, detecting main points, premise, and conclusions, and recognizing assumptions and missing assumptions. LSAT Arguments set up ideas and proceed to support them, often inadequately. For the Logical Reasoning/Argument sections, the LSAT experts recommend that you read the question first and then read the passage presented. The question will direct you to identify what is important in the passage. Also, understanding the structure of the Arguments questions declaws them. Having a sense of the structure gives you a focus, and a basis to understand a passage that is not going to be a fun read on your best day. The various LSAT experts agree that the following Argument style questions commonly appear on the LSAT.

1. Recognizing the author's main conclusion.

2. Identifying the author's main premise.

3. Identifying an implicit assumption of an argument underpinning a conclusion.

4. Recognizing evidence versus opinion.

5. Detecting flawed reasoning.

6. Understanding how additional facts change a conclusion.

91. The Premise Argument Question

The *Princeton Review* offers a good basic approach for analyzing a premise Argument question.

First, read the question to efficiently focus on the Argument.

Analyze the Argument to locate the author's conclusion and the evidence that supports it.

This means identifying what is relevant to the question, and avoiding the proverbial red herrings. If you can find the answer as you read the Argument, it will be easier to find the correct choice in the possible answers provided.

For some questions in the LSAT Logical Reasoning/Argument sections, no one answer will be clear. With those questions, you are tasked with selecting the best of the bad answers. Evaluate the choices given, and test them against the statements in the Argument relevant to the question asked.

This is the approach explained in the olive oil to heart disease relationship example discussed earlier. The author had drawn a conclusion about olive oil's reduction of heart disease; the question asked you to identify a statement that refuted that conclusion.

92. Understand the Role of Assumption

A second type of question often included in the LSAT Logical Reasoning/Argument section requires you to recognize and apply assumptions. While an assumption can sound or look deceptively like a premise, the difference is a premise is stated firmly as a fact; an assumption is taken to be true without proof. An LSAT Logical Reasoning/Argument question may ask you to identify an unstated assumption in the writer's reasoning — you are looking for supporting evidence that is not expressly stated in the passage. In reaching the stated conclusion the writer has assumed it inherently. This will be evident because the conclusion is not supported completely by the stated premises.

LSAC explains that generally it uses two types of assumptions in the LSAT Logical Reasoning/Argument questions: the necessary assumption and the sufficient assumption. A necessary assumption has to be true for the conclusion to work. A sufficient assumption is one that fills in a gap to expressly complete the reasoning process for the conclusion. LSAC advises that an assumption could be both necessary and sufficient. Is this clear as mud? Consider the following example of an assumption question quoted from Nova's *Master the LSAT*:

> "*Explorers of the northern regions in the early 1700s observed the natives playing an instrument similar to the mandolin. The instrument was strung with horse hair. Horses were not introduced into the New World until the 1500s. Thus, we can conclude that natives developed the instrument sometime between the introduction of the horses to the New World and the time of the explorers in the early 1700s.*"

Question: "Which one of the following assumptions is critical to the passage's conclusion?

    (A) Natives used the mandolin like instrument in all their religions practices.

    (B) Using horse hair in the mandolin-like instrument was one of the natives' earliest uses of horse hair.

    (C) This instrument was used by natives throughout North America.

    (D) Since it was first developed, the instrument was made with horse hair.

    (E) Explorers in the 1700s were the first to document natives' use of horse hair."

Commentary: To break open this question, you must be able to quickly recognize the stated premise from the conclusion. The conclusion is announced by the signpost words, "Thus we can conclude…" There are no premises stating that the natives did not have the instrument prior to the introduction of the horse. Therefore, inherent in the conclusion is the assumption that the natives did not develop this instrument until they had horse hair, as opposed to having previously used some other material before they had horses. Therefore, the assumption that is necessary for the conclusion is the one expressed in (D).

Another assumption type Logical Reasoning/Argument question is the following, which appeared on LSAC's Official LSAT PrepTest 32, October 2000 (Form OLSS47, Section 1, No. 5):

> "In some countries, there is a free flow of information about infrastructure, agriculture, and industry, whereas in other countries, this information is controlled by a small elite. In the latter countries, the vast majority of the population is denied vital information about factors that determine their welfare. Thus, these countries are likely to experience more frequent economic crises than other countries do."

Question: "The Conclusion follows logically if which one of the following is assumed?

(A) It is more likely that people without political power will suffer from economic crises than it is that people in power will.

(B) Economic crises become more frequent as the amount of information available to the population about factors determining its welfare decreases.

(C) In nations in which the government controls access

to information about infrastructure, agriculture, and industry, economic crises are common.

(D) The higher the percentage of the population that participates in economic decisions, the better those decisions are.

(E) A small elite that controls information about infrastructure, agriculture, and industry is likely to manipulate that information for its own benefit."

Commentary: The conclusion is highlighted by the signpost word: "Thus..." Note the wording of the key premise preceding the conclusion: "the vast majority of the population is denied vital information about factors that determine their welfare." Linked to that premise is the conclusion of "more frequent economic crises." Of the answers given, (B) is most closely aligned in language and most logically fits as a sufficient, assumption that economic crises become more frequent as information available to the population "about factors determining its welfare decreases." Therefore, (B) is the correct answer for the missing assumption. It is possible another assumption could fit, but there are no facts to support any but the one in (B) that closely tracks the language already provided in the passage. By comparison, in the horsehair musical instrument example, only one assumption makes the conclusion valid, and therefore that assumption was a necessary one.

93. Identify Flawed Arguments — False Premise

A third type of question often encountered in the Logical

Reasoning/Argument section is identifying the flaw in the author's reasoning. Most often this will be revealed as the author having missed something, which, if it were recognized, would undermine or negate the author's conclusion. Consider the following example:

> "The promoter of a condo development has petitioned the rural township trustees for a variance allowing the development to be located on a nearly defunct golf course abutting several homes and farmlands along two roads adjacent to the golf course. The developer has pointed out in the trustee meetings that the 112 units will be built according to an upscale design that will increase tax values for the local school district, and bring construction jobs to the local flagging economy. Accordingly, the trustees conclude that the development plan presents a good improvement for the township."

Question: Which of the following, if true, would undermine the wisdom of the trustees' conclusion about the development?

(A) The golf course would need to be upgraded.

(B) There is no water or sewer infrastructure available to serve the 112 unit utility demands and the development plans have not mentioned these services.

(C) The developer has not yet sold commitments for the units.

(D) The developer does not live in the township.

(E) The adjoining landowners have objected to the plan.

Commentary: If you read the question before the passage, you would be looking for what the trustees were missing in their consideration of the developer's proposal. The absence of water to 112 units, and sewer to carry away waste, should have immediately alerted you and the trustees as a flaw in the Argument. The objections of the adjoining landowners might be of some concern, but they are not necessarily on point to the developer's plan itself; the statement does not include evidence that their objections are sufficient to nullify the trustees' consideration. The flaw of missing water and sewer in the plan itself, on the other hand, is directly on point. The other answers do not have a bearing on the success of the project because they are ancillary to the developer's actual plan or are premature. The upgrading of the golf course and obtaining sales commitments would not be viable until approval for the go-ahead was obtained; where the developer lives contains no evidence that his residency is a requirement. The utilities issue is clearly stated, and has a direct bearing on the trustees' involvement or perspective as the public authority. Housing needs water and waste disposal. The "best" answer, therefore, is (B).

94. Identify the Unstated True Premise

Another type of Logical Reasoning/Argument question that is the converse of the above is one which asks you to detect an unstated premise that actually strengthens the conclusion reached by accurately choosing the unstated premise from among the possible answers. Consider the following hypothetical.

A local news reporter had a scoop that reporters dream of. He discovered the mayor of the town was involved in a money laundering scheme involving a massage parlor and a drug ring. The mayor's wife and son, who were not involved in the criminal activity, were present on the scene when the FBI executed a search warrant at the mayor's home, and made arrests with the reporter in tow thanks to an informant friend with the FBI. The news reporter took photos of the surprised mayor, and of the weeping wife hugging her teenage son in her arms. The reporter wrote down what everyone said. He hurried back to the paper to write the story and prepare the photos for the front page. But sometimes even a newsman has a heart. Looking at the photos as they spread across his desk, he saw the pain and suffering on the faces of the wife and son, so the reporter pulled the wife and son's photos. He submitted only the mayor and the FBI photos to editorial and he omitted any mention of the wife and son in his article, except to say they were not involved in the criminal scheme.

Question: Which of the following best strengthens this Argument?

(A) The reporter believed a real part of the story was the contrast of the venality of the mayor's criminal acts against the innocence and betrayal of his family.

(B) The reporter believed people would be angry if he reported about the wife.

(C) The reporter thought the real story was about the mayor anyway.

(D) The reporter liked the mayor's wife.

(E) The wife was going to be running for mayor.

Commentary: The point — the buried conclusion — of the passage is the newsman having a heart as the reason for pulling the photos of the wife and son giving them only a brief mention in his article. The positive unstated premise in the answers that supports the question is a noble act. A sacrifice of a guy with a heart is (A) because (A) indicates that he has given up an aspect of the story that has some sensationalistic punch. He could cash- in on the situation and use it to play up the criminality of the mayor's activities against the backdrop of his family's misery. Without the wife and son, the story loses something, and with it, the reporter loses something; his nobler selfless motivation has a cost. The other possible answers given do not support the newsman's higher valor, nor are there any facts to suggest they are a premise that fits; thus, they do not fit the paradigm as a missing premise.

95. Effectively Practicing the Games

The Analytical Reasoning section of the LSAT contains the Games questions. These are often the most troubling for many people until they learn to deconstruct them. As many as a half-dozen questions in this test section can be based on a single set of order and spatial relationships among several people or things. The football game carpool hypothetical mentioned earlier is a relatively simple example. There also may be conditional statements involved. An example of a conditional statement is "if it is raining it must be Tuesday."

The Games problems in the LSAT's Analytical Reasoning section commonly are constructed in three parts: premise, followed by a set of conditions or rules, followed by a series of questions that call for deductive reasoning to choose the one (and only one) response that correctly answers the question. The various help sources on the LSAT Games agree that the following are important rules for a calm approach to these word salads.

- Do not rush — steady is the beat to follow in this game.

- Take an initial half-minute or so to scan the test section so that you can begin with the one that seems easiest to you.

- Keep moving; you have prepared for this; work the games methodically in the way you have practiced these kinds of problems.

- Visualize the scene and draw a diagram or sketch representing the scenario; like the boxes for the three cars in the football carpool example.

- List the players beside your diagram; any that have a fixed location according to the rules can be placed in position, as we did with Jane in the football carpool example, and Candy who only worked on Friday in Ye Olde Shoppe question.

- Diagram the relationships using a notation that makes sense for you; you will practice this in your preparation tests.

- Assess the type of questions asked about the Game.

- Eliminate obvious incorrect answers.

Consider the following hypothetical set of Analytical Reasoning/Games questions that are similar to what you may find on the LSAT. Work through them and then review the commentary that follows:

- Eight horses – A, B, C, D, E, F, G, and H need to be housed in two barns. Barn 1 has 3 stalls; Barn 2 has 5 stalls. The stalls in each barn are lined up side by side

- A, B, C, D, E are mares

- F, G, H are stallions

- No stallion can be placed next to A or E

- A stallion cannot be placed beside a stallion

- F and G cannot be in the same barn

- H and G cannot be in the same barn

- A and B cannot be next to each other

- D and E cannot be next to each other

- C and E cannot be in the same barn

- B and D cannot be next to each other

- Only one horse can occupy one stall.

Question No. 1: If G is in Barn 1, which of the following horses should be housed in Barn 2?

(A) E

(B) B

(C) C

(D) G

(E) A

Question No. 2: Assume the stalls in Barn 1 are numbered consecutively 1 through 5, starting with 1 on the left end as you stand facing the stalls. G is in Barn 1 with A, B, D, and E. If G is in stall 4, in which stall is A?

(A) 1 or 5

(B) 3

(C) 2

(D) 1 or 2

(E) 5

Question No. 3: Which of the following arrangements will not work in Barn 1?

(A) B-G-D-A-E

(B) E-A-D-G-B

(C) A-D-G-B-E

(D) E-B-G-D-A

(E) None of the above.

Question No. 4: After stabling the horses for a few days the stable manager has discovered that A and E cannot be stabled next to each other in Barn 1. The Manager can resolve this problem by moving the horses to which of the following arrangements and still keep them all in Barn 1?

(A) A-D-E-G-B

(B) G-B-A-E-D

(C) E-A-D-B-A

(D) A-D-G-B-E

(E) A-E-G-D-B

Setting up the problem: This is a linear ordering and grouping game. The premise and rules set can be easily sketched for a diagram to assist you. Your diagram and notes might look like this, with "m" meaning mare and "s" meaning stallion.

Barn 1   Barn 2

A(m)	B(m)	C(m)	D(m)	E(m)	F(s)	G(s)	H(s)

Question No. 1: If G is in Barn 1, which of the following horses can be housed in Barn 2?

(A) E

(B) B

(C) C

(D) G

(E) A

Commentary: Applying the rules, stallions F and H cannot be in the same barn as G. Therefore, if G is in Barn 1, you know that F and H have to be in Barn 2. Yet, neither F nor H is given as a possible answer to the question. Also, F and H cannot be side-by-side in Barn 2 because the rules state that stallions cannot be next to each other. If you diagram this, it might look like the following:

Barn 1   Barn 2

A(m)	B(m)	C(m)	D(m)	E(m)	F̶(̶s̶)̶	G(s)	H̶(̶s̶)̶

You must determine which of those horses given as choices to Question No. 1 can be in Barn 2, according to the relationship rules. Which of the horses listed in the answers to Question No. 1 is compatible with F and H, both stallions? Looking at the possible answers, you can immediately eliminate (D)-G. G is a stallion and you already know he is in Barn 1. According to the rules, of the five mares, only C or D can be next to a stallion. On that basis, either C or D is eligible for Barn 2. But there is an additional rule; C cannot be in the same barn as E, and you already know that E has to be in Barn 1 because E cannot be next to a stallion and two of three horses in Barn 2 are F and H — stallions. Therefore, C must be the horse assigned to Barn 2. (C)-C is the correct answer.

Barn 1   Barn 2

A(m)	B(m)	C̶(̶m̶)̶	D(m)	E(m)	F̶(̶s̶)̶	G(s)	H̶(̶s̶)̶

Question No. 2. Assume the stalls in Barn 1 are numbered consecutively 1 through 5, starting with 1 on the left end as you stand facing the stalls. G is in Barn 1 with A, B, D, and E. If G is in stall 4 what are the options for placing A?

(A) 1 or 5

(B) 3

(C) 2

(D) 1 or 2

(E) 5

Commentary: Diagram the five stalls, numbered 1 through 5 and place G in the box numbered 4. The question asks where to place A. According to the rules, A cannot be next to a stallion. Therefore, any answer including stall 3 or 5 can be eliminated, as those stalls are next to G; this leaves either (C) or (D) as a possible answer. Both contain 2, indicating that stall 2 is assuredly one possibility. So, you only have to test stall 1 to see if that position also works. Using a diagram for Barn 1, place A in stall 1 and G in stall 4.

1	2	3	4	5
A	E	B	G(S)	D

According to the rules, E cannot be next to a stallion, so E has to be placed in stall 2. B and D can be placed by a stallion, but D cannot be placed by E. B can be placed by E. Therefore, the rules permit the arrangement with A in stall 1, and the best answer is (D) 1 or 2.

Question No. 3: Which of the following arrangements will not work in Barn 1?

(A) B-G-D-A-E

(B) E-A-D-G-B

(C) A-D-G-B-E

(D) E-B-G-D-A

(E) None of the above

This question tests if you are paying attention. If you look at the sequences in each answer, you should see that (A) and (B) are the same; one is the flip of the other. Likewise, (C) and (D) are also the flip of each other. No one of them, therefore, can be the one arrangement that will not work, so, without the need for further consideration, the answer must be "(E) None of the above."

Question No. 4: After stabling the horses for a few days, the stable manager has discovered that A and E cannot be stabled next to each other either. The manager can resolve this problem by moving the horses to which of the following arrangements in Barn 1?

(A) A-D-E-G-B

(B) G-B-A-E-D

(C) E-A-D-B-A

(D) A-D-G-B-E

(E) A-E-G-D-B

Commentary: There are a couple of ways of resolving this one. Any of the answers that show A and E side-by-side are immediately eliminated. These are (B), (C), and (E). Of the two remaining answers, if you apply the rules, you will find the one that works is (D). There is another way, though, that is even quicker. In Question No. 3, you had two configurations of the same horses in the same barn, each of which had to be right according to the way the question and answers are presented. Now that A and E cannot be next to each other, the sequence stated in (A) and (B) in Question No. 3 no longer works. All you have to do is look at the sequence in (C)/(D) of Question No. 4. If it still works with the additional rule (and it does), that same sequence appears as answer (D) in Question No. 4. Instead of testing three possible answers, you only have to test one, shaving time off the question. Although LSAC designs each question to stand alone, in this set of questions, one question does provide an opportunity to relate one to another.

The above set of four Analytical Reasoning/Games questions demonstrates that it may not be necessary to test every permutation possible in an Analytical Reasoning/Games question; frankly, it could cost you unnecessary time. The logic required is directed not only by the question but the possible answers given to the question. Notice that more than one operation of logic is imbedded in these questions. There is the logic of possible spatial arrangements under the rules of the scenario presented in the question, and there is another application of logic in play in analyzing the potential answers.

It is recommended that in the Analytical Reasoning/Games section question sets, you not fill in your chosen bubbles on the answer sheet until you have completed an entire set of questions. This is especially important when the set is like the above example where the questions intertwine.

When you have finished your four answers to this set of four questions, you would turn to the answer sheet and complete the corresponding bubbles. This approach allows you to stay focused through the entire set, which is a more efficient use of your time. As you fill in the answers to the set on the answer sheet, you are taking a mental break — a transition — before moving on to the next set. Also, it is a good moment to take a deep breath, hold it, exhale, and roll your shoulders or perform an isometric to clear your mind for the next problem. These are things that consume only a few seconds, but they are seconds which may actually improve your overall time on this section of the test.

The above practice set of questions illustrates test-taking techniques and also interpretation of the logic questions. It is important to (1) diagram the relationships for easy reference to the rules, (2) read the question, and (3) read the answers before leaping into the solutions.

Staying with the horses, consider the following set, based in part on a type of Game proposed in Nova's *Cracking the LSAT*.

"Six horses, A-B-C-D-E-F, are entered in a horse show class. The Judge has 4 ribbons to award in the class. Here is what you know about the horses and the ribbons awarded."

- 4 of the horses are geldings.

- 2 of the horses are mares.

- Each of the horses is either a Morgan or an Arabian, but not both.

- Both mares get a ribbon.

- One of the mares is a Morgan.

- Only one Morgan wins a ribbon.

- A and C place ahead of D.

- D places ahead of B and E.

- A and C are Morgans.

- D and F are Arabians.

Question No. 1: If E wins 4th place, which of the following must be true?

(A) A is a gelding.

(B) B is a gelding.

(C) E is a gelding.

(D) B is an Arabian.

(E) E is an Arabian.

Commentary: This is a hybrid question of an assignment Game. The central element is the horse to which there are three characteristics you have to assign; gender, mare, and gelding; breed — Morgan and Arabian; and placement in the class — 1st through 4th with no placement available for 2 of them. One neat diagram will not lay this type of problem out for you. The best you can do is sketch out a who's who based on what you have as you work through the questions. For example, you can lay out the order of class placement for four horses that you know from the rules given you in the premises; this gives you a starting reference point. The question states that E is in 4th place. Using the ordering rules given, you can list the known horses in order as follows:

A / C — D — E / B

This puts B in 5th place. The rules state that both mares won ribbons and B is a gelding; meaning that (B) B is a gelding is the correct answer to this question.

96. Effective Reading Comprehension

There is no one special key to approach Reading Comprehension, except to self-evaluate and improve your speed without sacrificing comprehension, focus, and accuracy. Most of the LSAT experts caution against "speed reading" in its normal meaning for this reason — they are right. You cannot speed read on the LSAT in the sense that you scan and miss half the words. Some sort of speed reading help may be necessary if you are a slower-than-average reader for a college graduate; it may help to work through the problem that is slowing you down. Barring that kind of a problem, you can increase your speed on the LSAT by practicing the LSAT questions on past tests.

For the Reading Comprehension section, some of the experts suggest that you scan the questions before reading the passages while others advise against it. Nova goes so far as to say that reading the questions first is a "cruel joke." The best advice is to do what proves to be consistently successful for you after you have taken several practice tests, and tried several techniques for yourself. Overall, the Reading Comprehension passages tend to be concentrated and detailed. The questions themselves are, by and large, just as densely composed. It is not going to cripple you to read the passage first to orient your thinking before further complicating your field of thought by reading the questions first. The following provides some examples of the types of Reading Comprehension questions you might encounter on the LSAT.

Reading Comprehension Passage

The "Organon" of Aristotle was a set of treatises in which Aristotle had written the doctrine of propositions. Study of these treatises was a chief occupation of young men when they passed from school to college, and proceeded from Grammar to Logic, the second of the Seven Sciences. Francis Bacon as a youth of sixteen, at Trinity College, Cambridge, felt the unfruitfulness of this method of search after truth. He was the son of Sir Nicholas Bacon, Queen Elizabeth's Lord Keeper, and was born at York House, in the Strand, on the 22nd of January, 1561. His mother was the Lord Keeper's second wife, one of two sisters, of whom the other married Sir William Cecil, afterwards Lord Burleigh. Sir Nicholas Bacon had six children by his former marriage, and by his second wife two sons, Antony and Francis, of whom Antony was about two years the elder. The family home was at York Place, and at Gorhambury, near St. Albans, from which town, in its ancient and its modern style, Bacon afterwards took his titles of Verulam and St. Albans.

Antony and Francis Bacon went together to Trinity College, Cambridge, when Antony was fourteen years old and Francis twelve. Francis remained at Cambridge only until his sixteenth year; and Dr. Rawley, his chaplain in after-years, reports of him that "whilst he was commorant in the University, about sixteen years of age (as his lordship hath been pleased to impart unto myself), he first fell into dislike of the philosophy of Aristotle; not for the worthlessness of the author, to whom he would ascribe all high attributes, but for the unfruitfulness of the way, being a

Reading Comprehension Passage

philosophy (as his lordship used to say) only strong for disputatious and contentions, but barren of the production of works for the benefit of the life of man; in which mind he continued to his dying day." Bacon was sent as a youth of sixteen to Paris with the ambassador Sir Amyas Paulet, to begin his training for the public service; but his father's death, in February, 1579, before he had completed the provision he was making for his youngest children, obliged him to return to London, and, at the age of eighteen, to settle down at Gray's Inn to the study of law as a profession. He was admitted to the outer bar in June, 1582, and about that time, at the age of twenty-one, wrote a sketch of his conception of a New Organon that should lead man to more fruitful knowledge, in a little Latin tract, which he called "Temporis Partus Maximus" ("The Greatest Birth of Time").

In November, 1584, Bacon took his seat in the House of Commons as member for Melcombe Regis, in Dorsetshire. In October, 1586, he sat for Taunton. He was member afterwards for Liverpool; and he was one of those who petitioned for the speedy execution of Mary Queen of Scots. In October, 1589, he obtained the reversion of the office of Clerk of the Council in the Star Chamber, which was worth 1,600 pounds or 2,000 pounds a year; but for the succession to this office he had to wait until 1608. It had not yet fallen to him when he wrote his "Two Books of the Advancement of Learning." In the Parliament that met in February, 1593, Bacon sat as member for Middlesex. He raised difficulties of procedure in the way of the grant of a treble subsidy, by just objection to the joining of the Lords with the Commons in a money grant, and a desire to extend the time allowed for payment from three years to six; it was, in fact, extended to four years. The Queen was offended.

Question 1: According to this passage Francis Bacon was by vocation:

(A) A follower

(B) An innovator

(C) An ambassador

(D) A courtier

(E) A lawyer

Question 2: Bacon's opinion of Aristotle is best described as:

(A) A dolt

(B) A philosopher disinterested in bettering mankind's quality of life

(C) A philosopher of flawed thinking

(D) Too ancient to have relevance to Bacon's day

(E) Not sufficiently argumentative to raise questions that would generate fruitful thought.

Commentary: The first question is one of those easier ones that LSAT sometimes throw into the mix, like a little puff of fresh air wafting through the test room. The passage tells you that Bacon "settled down" for the study of law at Gray's Inn. Indeed, his activities described while he served as a member of Parliament in the ensuing years speak of lawyer-like endeavors. The answer is (E) a lawyer. The other possible answers do not come close. The too-quick reader might grab the word "ambassador" from the passage where it mentions that Bacon accompanied the ambassador to France.

Less obvious than the first, the second question is not terribly difficult either. In this one, (A) is a quick throwaway and easily eliminated. It is clear in the passage that Bacon thought highly of Aristotle but only for "disputatious and contentions," which quickly eliminates (E) as well, which states the opposite concept. Still, (E) could trap the hurrying test taker, because at the beginning of the passage, there is a sentence referring to Bacon's view of the "unfruitfulness" of reading Aristotle's propositions as a "method of search after truth." This is why the LSAT experts are not comfortable with the notion of speed reading. If you catch the word "fruitful" coupled with "Aristotle," and seize on them as a link to (E), while missing the subtlety of the word "not" in answer (E), you may be drawn to it as the right answer and miss the question.

Moving on, nothing in the passage suggests Bacon thought Aristotle "too ancient," so (D) is easily eliminated as well. With (B) and (C) remaining, (B) becomes the best choice. The passage clearly states that Bacon disliked Aristotle's failure to contribute works, a "barrenness," to benefit the "life of man." (B) is square on to this thought; the notion of Aristotle having flawed thinking is not. Nothing in the passage suggests that Bacon thought Aristotle to be guilty of flawed thinking. To the contrary Bacon respected Aristotle's thinking.

Now consider the following passage in terms of Reading Comprehension analysis.

Reading Comprehension Passage

The three things essential to all wealth production are land, labor, and capital.

"The dry land" was created before there appeared the man, the laborer, to work it. With his bare hands the worker could have done nothing with the land either as a grazer, a farmer or a miner. From the very first he needed capital, that is, the tools to work the land.

The first tool may have been a pole, one end hardened in the fire, or a combined hoe and axe, made by fastening with wythes, a suitable stone to the end of a stick; but no matter the kind of tool, or the means of producing it, it represented capital, and the man who owned this tool was a capitalist as compared with the man without any such appliance.

From the land, with the aid of labor and capital, comes wealth, which in a broad way may be defined as something having an exchangeable value.

Reading Comprehension Passage

Before the appearance of money all wealth changed hands through barter. The wealth in the world to-day is immeasurably greater than all the money in it. The business of the world, particularly between nations, is still carried on through exchange, the balances being settled by money.

Money is a medium of exchange, and should not be confounded with wealth or capital; the latter is that form of wealth which is used with labor in all production.

Broadly speaking, wealth is of two kinds, dormant and active. The former awaits the development of labor and capital; the latter is the product of both.

Labor is human effort, in any form, used for the production of wealth. It is of two kinds — skilled and unskilled. The former may be wholly mental, while the latter may be wholly manual.

The successful farmer must be a skilled laborer, no matter the amount of his manual work. The unskilled farmer can never succeed largely, no matter how hard he works.

Trained hands with trained brains are irresistible.

Too many farmers live in the ruts cut by their great-great-grandfathers. They still balance the corn in the sack with a stone.

Farming is the world's greatest industry. All the ships might be docked, all the factory wheels stopped, and all the railroads turned to streaks of rust, and still the race would survive, but let the plow lie idle for a year and man would perish as when the deluge swept the mountain tops.

The next census will show considerably over 6,000,000 farms in the United States. Farming is the greatest of all industries, as it is the most essential. Our Government has wisely made the head of the Department of Agriculture a cabinet officer, and the effect on our farming interest is shown in improved methods and a larger output of better quality.

The haphazard, unskilled methods of the past are disappearing. Science is lending her aid to the tiller of the soil, and the wise ones are reaching out their hands in welcome.

Question No. 1: The author of this passage would not agree with which of the following statements?

(A) Land is the source of all wealth.

(B) Money is equal to barter.

(C) Capital can be expressed in terms of money.

(D) Dormant wealth is activated by labor.

(E) Property is essential to create capital.

Question No. 2: The author is arguing that:

(A) This county was built on the labor movement, without which there would be no capital

(B) Farmers must be skilled and use scientific methods to improve their quality and quantity of produce

(C) Without farmers civilization will come to an end

(D) The labor of farmers keeps civilization going

(E) This country is in danger of losing its agricultural base if we do not wake up and improve our farming methods.

Question No. 3: Which of the following is the author LEAST likely to agree with?

(A) Idle hands will not create capital.

(B) Some farmers are behind the times.

(C) Without money there can be no capital.

(D) Without capital there can be no money.

(E) Property is wealth.

Question No. 4: Which of the following best states the theme of the passage?

(A) Shipping supports agriculture.

(B) The cabinet office of Department of Agriculture proves the importance of Agriculture.

(C) Farming is our greatest industry, and therefore we must support the improvement of farming methods.

(D) We do not need money to live but we do need food and should support the farmers for better quality of produce.

(E) Barter is as good as money.

Commentary: Question No. 1 is a true-false type question asking you to interpret the author's viewpoints as presented in the possible answers to the question. In terms of difficulty, this is a fairly easy question. The author has clearly stated that capital is more than money, so (C) is the correct answer.

Question No. 2 asks you to locate the author's argument in the passage. When you read the passage, did you find that the author seemed to be making an argument? Indeed, the passage is slanted to be expressing and supporting a point of view about the importance of agriculture in more than just an academic sense, because the author notes that not all farmers are equal. Some appear to be lagging behind in terms of keeping up with scientific methods that will improve quality and quantity of produce. The author's discussion about the importance of agriculture above all other industries is presented in support of that premise to be persuasive. This is a question where more than one answer appears to speak to the author's point in this regard; both (B) and (E) are enticing. (E) is not truly supported by the evidence presented in the passage. The author does not state that he believes the agricultural base of the economy is in danger. To the contrary, the author mentions the encouraging census report of the number of farmers and the fact that the government recognizes agriculture as being worthy of its own cabinet office. The thrust of the passage is not that the world is coming to an end, but rather farming is what enables it to continue; that it will continue much better if farmers reach out for the improvements available to enhance their produce, improving the fruits of their labor. Therefore (B) is the correct answer for this question.

Question No. 3 is another true-false question asking you to interpret the author's viewpoint according to his statements. As you move down the list of answers, you should stop at (C) and move no further. One of the author's premises is that money has no place in the definition of capital. (C) is the correct answer to this question.

Question No. 4 is a recognition-of-theme question. This is one of those questions where you might read all of the answers, scratch your head, and not like any of them. Remember the LSAT adage — choosing the best of bad answers? For this question, you may safely eliminate (A) and (E). The author would most likely agree with these statements, but they are not clearly stated in the passage, and certainly are not relevant to the central discussion of the role of agriculture in the economy. (B) can be eliminated as an evidentiary statement in support of the author's primary theme of agriculture's importance in the economy, which leaves you a choice between (C) and (D). This is a hypothetical question and not taken from a real past LSAT — LSAC's opinion on this question is not available. Yet, based on how LSAC and the experts have explained the analysis of questions like this one, the best answer is (C), for the following reasons. Both (C) and (D) state the need to support improved farming methods. (D) states flatly that we do not need money to live which is not exactly what the author has stated in the passage. Rather, the author has stated that money is a secondary, even perhaps a tertiary, method of economic exchange dependent upon the existence of solid goods and services: property and labor. More importantly, (C) closely quotes the author's words from the passage stating that farming is our "greatest industry." This is an example of the type of clues a question may contain that will direct you to the right answer on the LSAT.

97. More Reading Comprehension/ Argument — 75% of the LSAT

After you have had the opportunity to work through several LSAT practice tests, you will begin to see that the singular difference between the Logical Reasoning/Arguments and the Reading Comprehension sections is the length of the passages — the latter being longer. With LSAC's advent of the comparative passages in the Reading Comprehension section, the demarcation between the two types of sections becomes even more blurred. Rather than consuming time to ponder the mysteries of how Logical Reasoning/Arguments differs from Reading Comprehension, understand that together these sections mean that 75 percent of the LSAT is about interpreting the English language in all its nuances, ambiguities, subtleties, double meanings, inferences, assumptions, subjective and objective impressions, and intentions inspired by the machinations of human thought and motivation. Were humans not so complex, and English not so fluid and plastic, jobs for lawyers would be more limited, and perhaps the LSAT would be less competitive.

Because 75 percent of the LSAT boils down to interpretation of often arcane and esoteric, densely constructed passages, which you must read and absorb swiftly in a compressed period of time, it makes sense to emphasize the Reading Comprehension sections in your preparation and improve your speed and interpretive skills. With this in mind, the following passages are provided for further practice and thought. These are not taken from any previous LSATs or practice tests. These are newly-constructed passages specifically for this book. They are either newly created by the author or adapted from literature and other writings in the public domain — the questions are original to this book. You will no doubt note that some of these passages are longer than those found on the Reading Comprehension sections of past LSAT tests. They are purposely so in order to challenge both your LSAT mental muscles and speed rate, and prepare you for longer LSAT innovations that could confront you on your particular Test Day.

The following statements are truisms about LSAT Reading Comprehension passages.

1. They are not selected for their scintillating, riveting interest.

2. They are often tedious.

3. They can be obscure, and even boring.

4. They are densely written; condensed in content, requiring close reading.

5. They are not uniformly organized in the same way, although overall you will find that patterns emerge; after all there are only so many ways to present text and ask questions.

6. They will be longer than your comfort level for the time constraints of the section.

7. Most of the questions will contain throwaway answers that are easily eliminated.

8. Facts will be laced with opinions.

9. Absolutes like "all," "every," "none," are seldom applicable concepts in the question structure.

10. The writer's opinion may not be yours. Do not be distracted.

Check your watch. Each Passage is followed by six questions. At the current going LSAT rate of 1.4 minutes per question, that is 8.4 minutes for each Passage set. The emphasis here, for purposes of your LSAT practice, is reading the passage and answering the questions within a set time limit. The correct answers are provided at the end. For each Passage, can you explain for yourself why the answers given are the best answers, and why the other answers are not the best answers?

Passage I

At 4:00 am on March 28, 1979, a serious accident occurred at the Three Mile Island 2 nuclear power plant near Middletown, Pennsylvania. The accident was initiated by mechanical malfunctions in the plant and made much worse by a combination of human errors in responding to it. During the next 4 days, the extent and gravity of the accident was unclear to the managers of the plant, to federal and state officials, and to the general public. What is quite clear is that its impact, nationally and internationally, has raised serious concerns about the safety of nuclear power. This Commission was established in response to those concerns. We examined with great care the sequence of events that occurred during the accident to determine what happened and why. We have attempted to evaluate the significance of various equipment failures as well as the importance of actions (or failures of actions) on the parts of individuals and organizations. We analyzed the various radiations releases and came up with the best possible estimates of the health effects of the accident. In addition, we looked more broadly into how well the health and safety of the workers was protected during normal operating conditions, and how well their health and safety and that of the general public would have been protected in the case of a more serious accident. We conducted an in-depth examination of the role played by the utility and its principal suppliers. We examined possible problems of organization, procedures, and practices that might have contributed to the accident. Since the major cause of the accident was due to inappropriate actions by those who were operating the plant and supervising that operation, we looked very carefully at the training programs that prepare operators and the procedures under which they operate. As requested by the President, we examined the emergency plans that were in place at the time of the accident. We also probed the responses to the accident by the utilities, by state and local governmental agencies in Pennsylvania, and by a variety of federal agencies. We looked for deficiencies in the plans and in their execution in order to be able to make recommendations for improvements for any future accident. In this process we had in mind how well the response would have worked if the danger to public health had been significantly greater. We examined the coverage of the accident by the news media. This was a complex process in which we had to separate out whether errors in media accounts were due to ignorance or confusion on the part of the official sources, to the way they communicated this information to the media, or to mistakes committed by the reporters themselves. We examined what sources were most influential on the people who needed immediate information, and how well the public was served by the abundant coverage that was provided. We also attempted to evaluate whether the coverage tended to exaggerate the seriousness of the accident either by selectively using alarming quotes more than reassuring ones, or through purposeful sensationalism. Finally, we spent a great deal of time

Passage I

on the agency that had a major role in all of the above: the Nuclear Regulatory Commission. The President gave us a very broad charge concerning this agency. We therefore tried to understand its complex structure and how well it functions, its role in licensing and rule making, how well it carries out its mission through its inspection and enforcement program, the role it plays in monitoring the training of operators, and its participation in the response to the emergency, including the part it played in providing information to the public. We took more than 150 formal depositions and interviewed a significantly larger number of individuals. At our public hearings we heard testimony by a wide variety of witnesses. We collected materials that fill 300 feet of shelves. Based on all materials we arrived at a number of major findings and conclusions. Based on these findings, this Commission made a series of recommendations. Each recommendation was approved by a majority of Commissioners.

It is just as important to understand what we did not do. We did not examine the entire nuclear industry. We did not look at military applications of nuclear energy. We did not consider nuclear weapons proliferation. We have not dealt with the question of the disposal of radioactive waste or the dangers of the accumulation of waste fuel. We have not attempted to evaluate the relative risks involved in alternative sources of energy. We did not attempt to reach a conclusion as to whether, as a matter of public policy, the development of commercial nuclear power should be continued or should not be continued. The improvement of the safety of existing and planned nuclear power plants is a crucial issue. It is this issue that our report addresses, those changes that can and must be made as a result of the accident — the legacy of Three Mile Island.

Question No. 1: The purpose of the Commission was to:

(A) Assess the emergency preparedness of the NRC and other governmental authorities.

(B) Develop a report of the history of commercial nuclear power in the United States.

(C) Report to the President why there was an accident at Three Mile Island.

(D) Investigate the accident at Three Mile Island and recommend safety changes in nuclear power plants as a result.

(E) Recommend a plan for shutting down nuclear power plants in the United States.

Question No. 2: The Commission received its charge and authority from:

(A) The Governor of Pennsylvania

(B) The United States Congress

(C) The President of the United States

(D) The Nuclear Regulatory Commission

(E) All of the above

Question No. 3: Which of the following best explains why the Commission examined coverage of the accident by the news media?

(A) Classified information was leaked to the news media.

(B) The President was unhappy about the news coverage.

(C) The Commission intended to impose a new blackout of its investigation of the Three Mile Island accident.

(D) There were errors in the news media accounts of the accident at Three Mile Island.

(E) The accident at Three Mile Island was far less serious than anyone was led to believe and was really a nonevent.

Question No. 4: Which of the following did the Commission not do?

(A) Analyze various radiation releases for health effects.

(B) Evaluate the NRC's role.

(C) Evaluate continuation of existing and planned nuclear power plants.

(D) Address improving safety of existing and planned nuclear power plants.

(E) Investigate Pennsylvania's emergency response plan.

Question No. 5: The Commission did not address the entire nuclear industry in its investigation because:

(A) Other studies were already working on other aspects of the nuclear industry.

(B) Its investigation was limited to Three Mile Island.

(C) It did not have enough time.

(D) It would have involved classified information to which it did not have access.

(E) The President told them not to.

Question No. 6: The opinion of the Commission according to this passage is that the accident at Three Mile Island was magnified by:

(A) Inefficiencies at the NRC

(B) Failure to file proper reports with the President

(C) Inherent failures of nuclear power plant safety measures

(D) Mechanical malfunctions

(E) Human errors

Passage II A

Advocates for passage of the anti-horse slaughter bill claim the time has come to stop an inhumane practice. Horse meat is not consumed in the United States. Horse by-products are no longer used in manufacture of goods. Horse meat is shipped overseas for consumption in foreign countries. There are only three operating horse rendering plants in the United States and the appalling conditions in these places are notorious. The practices and standards are abominable and everyone knows it. Because the meat is not lawfully controlled for consumption here nobody cares. Horses are ill-treated, sick, screaming in fear and pain, crammed into shipping vans with no air to breathe, mares often in foal or with foals by their side. Even worse, the brokers who sell these horses to the plants, known as the "killers," misrepresent themselves at auctions and even as personal buyers to people who sell their horses, sometimes in stressful situations due to financial hardship. Believing they are selling their horses to a good home, they send their beloved friends off instead to the killers, having no knowledge of what they have done or what torture awaits their friends. Horses are companions and pets in this country and should be respected as such. The inhumane butchering and torture must be stopped and cruelty for the reward of a few dollars put to a final end with federal penalties that have teeth in them.

Those who advocate total shut down of the remaining horse rendering plants in the United States ignore several problems that such action will create and the service these plants provide. What is needed instead is better regulation of the practices connected with these plants. There is a surplus of broken, ill and unwanted horses in this country. The horse rendering plants provide a solution of disposal, harsh

Passage II B

though it may seem, for such animals, who are not leading a quality or satisfactory life where they are. They are not being cared for if they are neglected, often left to fend for themselves where there is inadequate water or food. Human neglect of the worst kind is cruelty far worse than death for these poor creatures. The rendering plants have provided a solution for disposing of these unwanted starved animals. If the plants are closed, where will they go? Who will feed them? Who will care for them? Where will funds for humane treatment come from? Further, a fact that is little recognized is the use of the non-edible portions, the organs, of the animals that are given over to equine research. For example, the Veterinary School at The Ohio State University has long been the recipient from a rendering plant of equine reproductive organs, such as stomach, pancreas, heart, liver, kidneys, and so forth, for preservation, research, and study for teaching of veterinary students. These organs must be harvested and immediately preserved quickly to be of educational use and study in the university lab. With the closure of the plant, this source of organs for study is cut off. The advocates for plant closure argue inhumane treatment of the animals in transport and at the plants prior to the horses' deaths. That issue can and should be addressed by legislation and better inspection and controls at the plants and over the transporters. That is the way the problem should be addressed, rather than closure of the plants.

Question No. 1. The point on which both authors agree is:

(A) It would be ideal if there were no rendering plants.

(B) Horses should not be killed.

(C) Horses should not be mistreated.

(D) Rendering plants serve no social purpose.

(E) Rendering plants would be OK if the horses were not mistreated at them.

Question No. 2: Passage II A's main premise is:

(A) All horse rendering plants should be closed as inhumane.

(B) All horse rendering plants should be closed as obsolete.

(C) All horse rendering plants should be closed because horse meat is not consumed in the United States.

(D) All horse rendering plants should be closed because only 3 are left and that is not enough to be economically viable.

(E) All horse rendering plants should be closed because transport is too costly.

Question No. 3: Passage II B's main argument against II A is:

(A) Horse organs are needed for research and teaching.

(B) The horse population needs culling.

(C) II A is simply an emotional argument.

(D) The horses do not know the difference anyway.

(E) The problem II A raises can be solved with improved inspection and tighter regulations.

Question No. 4: Which of the following is most likely to be II A's response to II B's argument?

(A) Regulations and inspections cannot watch every hour, every day, and they will not change the people who are committing the atrocities against these horses.

(B) The overpopulation of horses can be directed to the veterinary schools instead of the rendering plants.

(C) There is no use for horse meat in the United States.

(D) There is no use for horse by-products in the United States.

(E) Horses are pets.

Question No. 5: Which of the following does II B fail to address in II A's argument?

(A) Horses are pets.

(B) The killers' misrepresentation of themselves to horse owners.

(C) The killers use inhumane tactics.

(D) Transport practices.

(E) Selection of animals for death at the plants.

Question No. 6: The fundamental difference between the viewpoints of II A and II B can be best described as which of the following?

(A) There is no difference. Both view the situation as requiring government control.

(B) II B believes horses should be used for science and II A does not.

(C) II A views horses as respected pets to be protected at a high standard of care and II B views them as property no different than other agricultural livestock.

(D) II A does not believe in any form of euthanasia for horses and II B does.

(E) II A is concerned about overpopulation of unwanted horses and II B is not.

Passage III

The following expresses a legal opinion to clarify issues surrounding the application of the Family and Medical Leave Act of 1993 (FMLA), 29 U.S.C. 2601 et seq., to an absence from work for the placement of a child for adoption or foster care. The issue concerns an employee who has a child placed in the home for foster care and then, after a period of one or more years, decides to adopt that same child. You question the FMLA regulation set forth at 29 CFR 825.201 that states, in part, "entitlement to leave for a birth or placement for adoption or foster care expires at the end of the 12-month period beginning on the date of the birth or placement...," and ask which placement date (for foster care or for adoption) qualifies the employee for leave entitlement or if both placement dates qualify for FMLA leave as separate events. You also inquire as to whether or not taking an adopted child on a vacation to introduce him/her to extended family can be a qualifying event under the FMLA.

The FMLA entitles eligible employees of covered employers to take up to 12 weeks of unpaid, job-protected leave each year – with continuation of group health insurance coverage under the same conditions as prior to leave and reinstatement to the same or equivalent position – for specified family and medical reasons. In answering your inquiry, we assume you refer to a covered employer, an eligible employee and that all other applicable criteria for FMLA leave have been met.

As you are aware, FMLA section 102(a)(1)(B) and the regulations at 29 CFR 825.112(a)(2) allow an eligible employee to take leave for the placement of a son or daughter with the employee for adoption or foster care. In addition, section 102(a)(2) of the Act provides that "[the entitlement to leave...for a birth or placement of a son or daughter shall expire at the end of the 12-month period beginning on the date of such birth or placement."

The regulations also discuss the timing of when an employee may use FMLA leave for purposes of adoption or foster care placements. Regulation 825.200(a) provides that an eligible employee's FMLA leave entitlement is limited to a total of 12 workweeks of leave during any 12-month period for, among other purposes, the "placement with the employee of a son or daughter for adoption or foster care, and to care for the newly placed child" (emphasis added). The regulation is based on the Act's

Passage III

legislative history, which similarly emphasizes that the leave is available to care for a "child newly placed with the employee for adoption or foster care." Senate Report No. 103-3, p.24. The statutory focus on the date of placement and the legislative history indicate that only the initial date of placement with a family triggers the right to leave.

In the scenario you provide, the child would be "newly placed" at the time of the foster care placement rather than when the subsequent adoption occurs. Therefore, only the placement for foster care would be a FMLA qualifying event.

You also ask whether taking an adopted child on vacation to meet extended family members constitutes a FMLA qualifying event. The FMLA does not require an employer to grant FMLA leave for the purpose of taking an adopted child on vacation to meet extended family. FMLA section 102(b) provides that leave taken for the placement of a son or daughter with the employee for adoption or foster care "shall not be taken by an employee intermittently or on a reduced leave schedule unless the employee and the employer of the employee agree otherwise." Intermittent leave is leave taken in separate blocks of time for the same FMLA-qualifying reason. In other words, FMLA leave for the placement of a child for foster care or adoption needs to be taken in one block of time, unless the employer and employee agree that the leave can be taken intermittently.

Nothing in the FMLA, however, prohibits the employee from introducing his or her newly placed son or daughter to extended family members while taking leave for the placement of the child. The initial placement of the child for adoption or foster care would be the qualifying event. While on leave for the placement, as a part of integrating the child into your employee's family, he or she could introduce the child to the extended family.

Question No. 1: In addressing the question posed about the FMLA the writer has assumed which of the following?

(A) The person seeking advice is eligible for coverage by FMLA.

(B) Congress has passed the FMLA.

(C) The President has signed the FMLA into law.

(D) Foster care is a qualifying event under FMLA.

(E) Adoption is a qualifying event under FMLA.

Question No. 2: Which of the following best states the writer's main conclusion?

(A) The person seeking advice is not eligible for FMLA leave.

(B) Meeting extended family is not a reason that qualifies to take time off for FMLA.

(C) The person cannot take FMLA for the adoption because it is not a new placement of that child.

(D) The person cannot use FMLA for foster care, but can use it for adoption.

(E) FMLA only provides covered leave for birth of the person's own natural child.

Question No. 3: The key premise for the writer's main conclusion is which of the following:

(A) The employer's vacation policy

(B) Information provided by the extended family

(C) Adoption or foster care is the qualifying event

(D) FMLA section 102(b)

(E) Regulation 825.200(a)'s provision of "newly placed" child

Question No. 4: The logical conclusion from this letter is:

(A) The parent of the adopted child cannot go on vacation.

(B) The employer has violated the parent's FMLA rights.

(C) The parent should be allowed to take intermittent leave for adoption if she did not use up the whole 12 weeks in her first 12 months since placement in foster care.

(D) FMLA leave was only available to the employee for 12 weeks during the first 12 months from the first day of new placement of the child in foster care with the employee.

(E) The employee's vacation can also be counted as FMLA leave.

Question No. 5: According to the opinion expressed in this letter which of the following must be true?

(A) A person covered by FMLA who takes foster placement of a child should wait to adopt the child before notifying the employer of wanting to take FMLA leave.

(B) A person covered by FMLA who takes foster placement of a child should take FMLA leave within 12 months following the initial placement of the child to acclimate the child to the family.

(C) A person covered by FMLA who takes foster placement of a child will not be eligible for FMLA leave until the child is officially adopted.

(D) Different rules for FMLA leave apply for the birth of an employee's own child than for foster care or adoption.

(E) The employee and employer can mutually agree to extend the 12 month time limit for foster care or adoption to a longer time period.

Question No. 6: Which of the following is a logical inference as to the purpose of the FMLA provision that is the subject of this letter?

(A) The 12-week block of time in the first year of the child's placement is intended to give the parent and child a chance to bond and get acquainted with each other and the rest of the family.

(B) The parent will be too tired from the strain of the new child to do a good job at work.

(C) The child will initially need special care.

(D) The law is necessary to accommodate single parent homes.

(E) The law will encourage families to adopt or take in foster children.

Passage IV

"I want to see Mr. John Barron, please."

The other laughed, as if this was an admirable jest.

"I suppose you do, though that's a queer way to put it. You talk as though you had come to smoke a cigar along with him."

Passage IV

In growing amazement and suspicion, Noy listened to this most curious statement. Fears suddenly awoke that, by some mysterious circumstance, Barron had learned of his contemplated action and was prepared for it. He stopped, therefore, looked about him sharply to avoid any sudden surprise, and put a question to the footman.

"You spoke as though I was wanted," he said. "What do you mean by that?"

"Blessed if you're not a rum 'un!," answered the man. "Of course you was wanted, else you wouldn't be here, would you? You're not a party as calls promiscuous, I should hope. Else it would be rather trying to delicate nerves. You're the gentleman as everybody requires some time, though nobody ever sends for himself."

Failing to gather the other's meaning, Noy only realized that John Barron expected some visitor and felt, therefore, the more determined to hasten his own actions. He saw the footman was endeavoring to be jocose, and therefore humored him, pretending at the same time to be the individual who was expected.

"You're a funny fellow and must often make your master laugh, I should reckon, Iss, I be the chap what you thought I was. An' I should like to see him—the guv'nor—at once if he'll see me."

The footman chuckled again.

"He'll see you all right. He's been wantin' of you all day, and he'd have been that dreadful disapp'inted if you 'adn't come. Always awful particular about his clothes, you know, so mind you're jolly careful about the measuring 'cause this overcoat will have to last him a long time."

Taking his cue from these words Noy, still ignorant of the truth, made answer: "Iss, I'll measure en all right. Wheer is he to?"

"In the studio—there you are, right ahead. Knock at that baize door and then walk straight in, 'cause he'll very likely be too much occupied to answer you. He's quite alone—leastways I believe so."

Noy put his revolver into the side pocket of his coat, and, following the footman's directions, pushed open the swing door, which yielded to his hand. Scanty light illuminated the studio from one oil lamp which hung by a chain from a bracket in the wall, and the rays of which were much dimmed by a red glass shade. Mostly empty easels stood about the sides of the great chamber; here and there on the white walls were sketches in charcoal and daubs of paint., Noy caught sight of an object which made him gasp violently and hurry forward. Alone under the lofty open windows

Passage IV

which rose on the northern side of the studio, stood a couch, and upon it lay a small, straight figure shrouded in white sheets save for its face.

John Barron had been dead twenty-four hours, and he had hastened his own end, by a space of time impossible to determine, through leaving his sick-room two days previously, that he might visit the picture gallery wherein hung "Joe's Ship." It was a step taken in absolute defiance of his medical men. The day of that excursion had chanced to be a very cold one, and during the night which followed it John Barron broke a blood vessel and precipitated his death. Now, in the hands of hirelings, without a friend to put one flower on his breast or close his dim eyes, the man lay waiting for an undertaker; and while Joe Noy glared at him, unconsciously gripping the weapon he had brought, it seemed as though the dead smiled under the red flicker of the lamp—as though he smiled and prepared to come back into life to answer this supreme accuser.

As by an educated mind Joe Noy's estimate and assurance of the eternal tortures of hell cannot be adequately grasped in its full force, so now it is hard to set forth with a power sufficiently luminous and terrific the effect of this discovery upon him. He, the weapon of the Almighty, found his work finished, the fruits of his labors snatched from his hand. His enemy had escaped, and the fact that he was dead only made the case harder. Disappointment beat upon his soul like a recurring wave, as thought drifted back and back, and told him that he had fairly won hell-fire and must abide by it.

So thinking, he returned to his lodging, entered unobserved and prowled the small chamber till dawn. By morning light all his life appeared transfigured and a ghastly anti-climax faced the man.

Question No. 1: The footman thought Noy to be John Barron's:

(A) Friend

(B) Lawyer

(C) Undertaker

(D) Relative

(E) Business associate.

Question No. 2: Noy arrived at Barron's to:

(A) Pay John Barron his respects

(B) Borrow money

(C) Propose a business proposition

(D) Steal a painting

(E) Kill John Barron.

Question No. 3: Which of the following best describes how Noy felt upon finding Barron dead?

(A) Thwarted

(B) Surprised

(C) Relieved

(D) Indifferent

(E) Afraid

Question No. 4: Which of the following best describes what the footman meant by the word "promiscuous?"

(A) Sexually indiscriminate

(B) Talks too much

(C) Rude

(D) Visits without invitation

(E) Hard of hearing

Question No. 5: A logical inference to draw from the passage about Noy is that:

(A) He is uneducated

(B) He is an aristocrat

(C) He is used to killing

(D) He is an atheist

(E) He is a relative of John Barron.

Question No. 6: A logical inference about John Barron is that:

(A) He had many friends.

(B) He committed suicide.

(C) He was ill and without friends when he died.

(D) He was an atheist.

(E) He feared God.

Passage V

Civilization, I apprehend, is nearly synonymous with order. However much we may differ touching such matters as the distribution of property, domestic relations, the law of inheritance and the like, most of us, I should suppose, would agree that without order civilization, as we understand it, cannot exist. Now, although the optimist contends that, since man cannot foresee the future, worry about the future is futile, and that everything, in the best possible of worlds, is inevitably for the best, I think it clear that within recent years an uneasy suspicion has come into being that the principle of authority has been dangerously impaired, and that the social system, if it is to cohere, must be reorganized. So far as my observation has extended, such intuitions are usually not without an adequate cause, and if there be reason for anxiety anywhere, it surely should be in the United States, with its unwieldy bulk, its heterogeneous population, and its complex government. After the American and French Revolutions and the Napoleonic wars, the industrial era opened, and brought with it a new governing class, as every considerable change in human environment must bring with it a governing class to give it expression. Perhaps, for lack of a recognized name, I may describe this class as the industrial capitalistic class, composed in the main of administrators and bankers. As nothing in the universe is stationary, ruling classes have their rise, culmination, and decline, and I conjecture that this class attained to its acme of popularity and power, at least in America, toward the close of the third quarter of the nineteenth century. I draw this inference from the fact that in the next quarter resistance to capitalistic methods began to take shape in such legislation as the Interstate Commerce Law and the Sherman Act, and almost at the opening of the 20th century a progressively rigorous opposition found for its mouthpiece the President Franklin Rocsevelt. History may not be a very practical study, but it teaches some useful lessons, one of which is that nothing is accidental, and that if men move in a given direction, they do so in obedience to an impulsion as automatic as gravity. Therefore, if Mr. Roosevelt became, as his adversaries say, an agitator, his agitation had a cause which is as deserving of study as is the path of a cyclone.

This problem has long interested me, and I harbor no doubt not only that the equilibrium of society very rapidly shifted, but that Mr. Roosevelt had, half-automatically, been stimulated by the instability about him to seek for a new centre of social gravity. In plain English, I infer that he concluded that industrialism had induced conditions which could no longer be controlled by the old capitalistic methods, and that the country must be brought to a level of administrative efficiency competent to deal with the strains and stresses of the twentieth century, just as this country resolved its first such problem by adopting the Constitution. Acting on these premises, whether consciously worked out or not, Mr. Roosevelt's next step was to begin the readjustment; but, I infer, that on attempting any correlated measures of reform,

Passage V

Mr. Roosevelt found progress impossible, because of the obstruction of the courts. To try to overleap that obstruction, and he suggested, without, I suspect, examining the problem very deeply, that the people should assume the right of "recalling" judicial decisions made in causes which involved the nullifying of legislation. What would have happened had Mr. Roosevelt been given the opportunity to thoroughly formulate his ideas, even in the midst of an election, can never be known, for greater global difficulties occupied him. Still, the inference that radical changes are at hand might be deduced from the past. In the experience of the English-speaking race, about once in every three generations a social convulsion has occurred; and probably such must continue to occur in order that laws and institutions may be adapted to physical growth. Human society is a living organism, working mechanically, like any other organism. It has members, a circulation, a nervous system, and a sort of skin or envelope, consisting of its laws and institutions. This skin, or envelope, however, does not expand automatically, as it would had Providence intended humanity to be peaceful, but is only fitted to new conditions by those painful and conscious efforts which we call revolutions. Usually these revolutions are warlike, but sometimes they are benign, as was the revolution over which General Washington, our first great "Progressive," presided, when the rotting Confederation, under his guidance, was converted into a relatively excellent administrative system by the adoption of the Constitution. Taken for all in all, I conceive General Washington to have been the greatest man of the eighteenth century, but to me his greatness chiefly consists in that balance of mind which enabled him to recognize when an old order had passed away, and to perceive how a new order could be best introduced. Even Washington could not alter the limitations of the human mind. He could postpone, but not avert, the impact of conflicting social forces. In 1789 he compromised, but could not determine the question of sovereignty. He eluded an impending conflict by introducing courts as political arbitrators, and the expedient worked more or less well until the tension reached a certain point. Then it broke down, and the question of sovereignty had to be settled in America, as elsewhere, on the field of battle. It was not decided until Appomattox. To attain his object, Washington introduced a written organic law, which of all things is the most inflexible. No other modern nation has to consider such an impediment.

Question No. 1: The writer's reference to Washington's postponement and Appomattox is a reference to:

(A) World War II

(B) World War I

(C) The War Between the States

(D) The War of 1812

(E) The Louisiana Purchase

Question No. 2: The writer's theme is best stated by which of the following statements?

(A) Capitalism has outlived its time.

(B) Roosevelt would have changed the Constitution if he had not been distracted.

(C) Washington would rewrite the Constitution if he were here today.

(D) The social order needs to be reorganized to insure survival of civilization.

(E) Washington saved the social order with the Constitution.

Question No. 3: With which of the following would the writer LEAST agree?

(A) Courts in 1789 were an expedient to balance political power in this country.

(B) Washington's brilliance in conceiving the concept of the Constitution in his day averted crisis and unified the states.

(C) The Constitution is an impediment today because it prevents change that is needed to maintain social order.

(D) The Constitution as an organic document is as viable today as it was in Washington's time.

(E) Roosevelt was a progressive who was thwarted from making innovations he might have done by having to deal with greater, pressing issues of his day.

Question No. 4: The writer would most likely agree with which of the following as an analogy to human society?

(A) An automobile.

(B) A factory.

(C) A snake that periodically must shed its skin.

(D) An island that grows from its own volcano.

(E) A phoenix that rises out of its own ashes.

Question No. 5: The writer seems to be most closely characterizing Franklin Roosevelt as a:

(A) Democrat

(B) Republican

(C) Libertarian

(D) Socialist

(E) Capitalist

Question No. 6: According to the passage, war is inevitable for change because:

(A) It is the only way to overcome the courts' decisions.

(B) The Constitution is inflexible.

(C) Providence did not intend humans to be peaceful.

(D) War always occurs every third generation.

(E) Political arbitration never works.

Passage VI

Thoughtful men, in every class, are not afraid of theology, i.e. of a reasoned account of their religion, but they want a theology which can be stated without conventions and technicalities; they do not at all care for a religion which pretends to do away with all mystery, but they are glad to be assured of the essential reasonableness of the Christian Faith; they do not expect a ready-made solution of the problem of evil, but they wish to see it honestly faced; above all, they want to know how Christian truth bears on the real problems of life; the best of them are not at all afraid of a religion which makes big demands on them, but they know well enough the difficulty of responding to those claims, and their greatest need of all is to find and to use that life and power, coming from a living Person, without which our best aspirations must fail and our highest ideals remain unrealized. GOD, if He exists at all, must obviously be important: and it is conceivable that He prefers the dogmatic atheism of a man here and a man there, or the serious agnosticism of a slightly larger number, to the practical indifference of the majority. "There are two attitudes, and only two, which are worthy of a serious man: to serve GOD with his whole heart, because he knows Him; or to seek GOD with his whole heart, because he knows Him not."

The ordinary Englishman is in most cases nominally a Christian. As a rule he has been admitted in infancy by baptism into the Christian Church. But he is ignorant of the implications of his baptism, and indifferent to the claims of a religion which he fails to understand. He is very apt to regard the Gospels conventionally. An inherited orthodoxy which has made peace with the world takes them for granted as a story

Passage VI

not unlike the way one reads a fairy tale. But if one really listens to the words told it becomes something more powerful. It is the portrait of One who spent the first thirty years of His life in an obscure Galilaean village, and who in early manhood worked as a carpenter in a village shop.

He first came forward in public in connection with a religious revival initiated by John the Baptist who baptized Him in the River Jordan. What His baptism meant to Him is symbolized by the account of a vision which He saw, and a Voice which designated Him as Son of GOD. He became conscious of a religious mission, and was at first tempted to interpret His mission in an unworthy way, to seek to promote spiritual ends by temporal compromises or to impress men's minds by an appeal to mystery or miracle. He rejected the temptation, and proclaimed simply GOD and His Kingdom. He is said to have healed the sick and to have wrought other "signs and mighty works": but He set no great store by these things, and did not wish to be known primarily as a wonder-worker.

He lived the life of an itinerate Teacher, declaring to any who cared to listen to the things concerning the Kingdom of GOD. At times He was popular and attracted crowds: but He cared little for popularity, wrapped up His teaching in parables, and repelled by His "hard sayings" all but a minority of earnest souls. He gave offence to the conventionalists and the religiously orthodox by the freedom with which He criticized established beliefs and usages, by His championship of social outcasts, and by His association with persons of disreputable life. Unlike John the Baptist, He was neither a teetotaller nor a puritan. He was not a rigid Sabbatarian. He despised humbug, hypocrisy, and cant: and He hated meanness and cruelty. He could be stern with a terrible sternness. His gaze pierced through all disguises, and He understood the things that are in the heart of man. He was never under any illusions.

He faced the hostility of public opinion with unflinching courage. He expected to be crucified, and crucified He was. He warned those who followed Him to expect a similar fate. He claimed from men an allegiance that should be absolute. He saw nothing inconsistent between this concentration of men's allegiance upon His own person, and His insistence upon GOD as the one great Reality that mattered.

The motive of His whole life was consecration to the will of GOD. He was rich towards GOD, where other men are poor. The words were true of Him, as of no one else, "I have set GOD always before me." He hated evil, because GOD hates it. He loved purity, because GOD is pure.

Passage VI

He loved children, the birds and the flowers, the life of the open air: but He was equally at home in the life of the town. He went out to dinner with anybody who asked Him: He rejoiced in the simple hilarity of a wedding feast. He was a believer in fellowship, and in human brotherhood. He was everybody's friend, and looked upon no one as beyond the pale. He loved sinners and welcomed them, without in the least condoning what was wrong. He looked upon the open and acknowledged sinner as a more hopeful person from the religious point of view than the person who was self-satisfied and smug. He said that He came to seek and to save those who knew themselves to be lost. If we will take seriously the human Jesus we shall discover in the end Deity revealed in manhood, and we shall worship Him in whom we have believed.

Question No. 1: Which of the following BEST evidences genuine religious belief according to the writer?

(A) Living life sincerely and actively according to Christ's example.

(B) Studying theology.

(C) Repudiating the devil.

(D) Recanting evil.

(E) Hating what God hates.

Question No. 2: Jesus' awakening to public life was:

(A) Prayer

(B) Marriage

(C) John the Baptist

(D) The Devil

(E) Baptism

Question No. 3: The writer views his peers' beliefs have:

(A) Become agnostic

(B) Strayed from the true Jesus

(C) Become devout

(D) Become dogmatic

(E) Met his expectations

Question No. 4: The best summary of the writer's view of Jesus is which of the following?

(A) He was a follower of John the Baptist.

(B) He was a brother of John the Baptist.

(C) He was a Jewish Prophet.

(D) He was a man who knew and loved God and brought God's message to people in simple and loving terms.

(E) He was God personified as a man.

Question No. 5: One of the main points about Jesus' example is:

(A) Attract followers with miracles

(B) Teach with parables

(C) Not allow faith to be swayed by public opinion

(D) Be a rigid Sabbatarian

(E) Seek popularity to spread faith

Question No. 6: From the writer's point of view the WORST point of view to have about religious faith is:

(A) Questioning

(B) Fear

(C) Disbelief

(D) Seeking

(E) Indifference

Passage VII A

Instead of seeing the all the different religions of the world as divisive we should recognize how similar each one is and how much they evidence transcendent unity of humanity. Every one of the great religions identify with a power, an energy, that is greater than humankind, something that we reach for to take us to a plane beyond the physical, that emphasizes a spiritual aspect of existence. Hindus believe this spiritual life essence is present in all living things. Without studying the biology of protoplasm or perhaps even understanding that such exists, they recognize that an indefinable spark of life transcends the physical anatomical elements that compose the most basic cell of life. Mohammed listened to the voice of God and exhorted his followers to remember five times a day that a power greater than they commands the universe. Christ preached a similar but far gentler message, and he opened his arms to all with the balm of forgiveness. Buddhists seek a higher level of being, the Way, beyond the cycle of death and suffering. Judaism follows the ancient laws of God as laid down by Moses and developed through the Talmud, a structured way of living and worshipping God through a devout belief system. None of these beliefs of something higher and better should be seen to conflict, but rather as unifying. They evidence that it is humankind's genetic structure to know and understand there exists a Higher Power to which we must give a name, and the name is, for most, God. They are

Passage VII A

also evidence that many paths lead to God. Were it not so, how else could we poor souls have a hope of finding our way to Him as we stumble about in the dark?

Passage VII B

Religion is the bane of civilization and the greatest fraud to ever be perpetrated on humanity. That the world was flat was an idea that at least made some sort of sense in its time. More wars have been fought in the name of religion and more torture has been committed in the name of "God" than any other concept known to humankind. For some reason I cannot divine, it is very important to every facet of humankind to impose its beliefs on the rest of humankind, as if thought were a property right. It is of course, a source of power having nothing to do with worship or goodness. Religion is a tool to control social groups. Convince a group of ever growing number of people to come together in a frenzy of worship, to hang on every word of a charismatic leader, and you will have an army ready to march into battle. To achieve a higher plane of peaceful existence, there must be an intellectual evolution that removes from the human race the need for religion. Otherwise we will continue to inevitably fall prey to following banners of false beliefs, like lemmings mindlessly careening toward the brink of extinction in the name of a faceless "god" that does not exist except in the lowest common denominator of human imagination.

Question No. 1: The underlying premise of Passage A is:

(A) All religions worship the same God.

(B) Protoplasm is evidence of God.

(C) The yearning for God is written into human DNA.

(D) One day all religions will merge into one.

(E) There will not be world peace until there is one worldwide religion.

Question No. 2: The underlying premise of Passage B is:

(A) Humankind has created the concept of religion to maintain power over social groups.

(B) There is no god.

(C) One day the world religions will merge into one.

(D) One day we will evolve by mutation so that God is no longer in our DNA.

(E) The only true religion is peace.

Question No. 3: Which of the following BEST states the likely response of Passage A's writer to Passage B's statement that religion is the cause of wars?

(A) War and religion have no connection with each other.

(B) War is in a different part of human DNA and cannot be blamed on religion.

(C) Humankind's quest for God is a seeking for a higher power beyond the lower physical plane of war, death and suffering.

(D) You cannot fight biology.

(E) War is physical, God is spiritual.

Question No. 4: Both writers have a point of agreement on which of the following:

(A) Most people are followers

(B) There is a Higher Power called God

(C) Religion is necessary for humanity

(D) Humanity seeks a higher plane of peaceful existence

(E) Religion is a farce.

Question No. 5: The writer of Passage B believes which of the following is TRUE?

(A) God is necessary for social order.

(B) Leaders have used God as a reason to make war.

(C) War is physical, God is spiritual.

(D) The need for God is in human DNA.

(E) Protoplasm is proof of God.

Question No. 6: The writer of Passage A would likely assume which of the following to be TRUE?

(A) The need for God is in our DNA; God put it there.

(B) Eventually humanity will evolve beyond the need for God.

(C) God is a creation of the human imagination.

(D)   God is an intellectual construct that leads to a higher plane through meditation.

(E) If humanity is unable to achieve the higher plane it will become extinct.

Passage VIII

This Commission was created to ascertain the facts relating to the assassination of President John Fitzgerald Kennedy in Dallas, Texas, on November 22, 1973. The Commission has addressed itself to this task and has reached certain conclusions based on all the available evidence. No limitations have been placed on the Commission's inquiry; it has conducted its own investigation, and all Government agencies have fully discharged their responsibility to cooperate with the Commission in its investigation. These conclusions represent the reasoned judgment of all members of the Commission and are presented after an investigation which has satisfied the Commission that it: has ascertained the truth concerning the assassination of President Kennedy to the extent that a prolonged and thorough search makes this possible.

The shots which killed President Kennedy and wounded Governor Connally were fired from the sixth floor window at the southeast corner of the Texas School Book Depository. This determination is based upon the following:

Witnesses at the scene of the assassination saw a rifle being fired from the sixth floor window of the Depository Building, and some witnesses saw a rifle in the window immediately after the shots were fired.

The almost whole bullet found on Governor Connally's stretcher at Parkland Memorial Hospital and the two bullet fragments found in the front seat of the Presidential limousine were fired from the 6.5- millimeter Mannlicher-Carcano rifle found on the sixth floor of the Depository Building to the exclusion of all other weapons.

The three used cartridge cases found near the window on the sixth floor at the southeast corner of the building were fired from the same rifle which fired the above-described bullet and fragments, to the exclusion of all other weapons.

The windshield in the Presidential limousine was struck by a bullet fragment on the inside surface of the glass, but was not penetrated.

The nature of the bullet wounds suffered by President Kennedy and Governor Connally and the location of the car at the time of the shots establish that the bullets were fired from above and behind the Presidential limousine, striking the President and the Governor.

There is no credible evidence that the shots were fired from the Triple Underpass, ahead of the motorcade, or from any other location. The weight of the evidence indicates that there were three shots fired.

Passage VIII

There is no question in the mind of any member of the Commission that all the shots which caused the President's and Governor Connally's wounds were fired from the sixth floor window of the Texas School Book Depository by Lee Harvey Oswald, based on the following:

The Mannlicher-Carcano 6.5-millimeter Italian rifle from which the shots were fired was owned by and in the possession of Oswald.

Oswald carried this rifle into the Depository Building on the morning of November 22, 1963.

Oswald, at the time of the assassination, was present at the window from which the shots were fired.

Shortly after the assassination, the Mannlicher-Carcano rifle belonging to Oswald was found partially hidden between some cartons on the sixth floor and the improvised paper bag in which Oswald brought the rifle to the Depository was found close by the window from which the shots were fired.

Based on testimony of the experts and their analysis of films of the assassination, the Commission has concluded that a rifleman of Lee Harvey Oswald's capabilities could have fired the shots from the rifle used in the assassination within the elapsed time of the shooting. The Commission has concluded further that Oswald possessed the capability with a rifle which enabled him to commit the assassination.

Oswald lied to the police after his arrest concerning important substantive matters.

Oswald had attempted to kill Maj. Gen. Edwin A. Walker (Retired, U.S. Army) on April 10, 1963, thereby demonstrating his disposition to take human life.

Oswald killed Dallas Police Patrolman J. D. Tippit approximately 45 minutes after the assassination. This conclusion upholds the finding that Oswald fired the shots which killed President Kennedy and wounded Governor Connally and is supported by the following:

Two eyewitnesses saw the Tippit shooting and seven eyewitnesses heard the shots and saw the gunman leave the scene with revolver in hand. These nine eyewitnesses positively identified Lee Harvey Oswald as the man they saw.

The cartridge cases found at the scene of the shooting were fired from the revolver in the possession of Oswald at the time of his arrest to the exclusion of all other weapons.

Passage VIII

The revolver in Oswald's possession at the time of his arrest was purchased by and belonged to Oswald.

Oswald's jacket was found along the path of flight taken by the gunman as he fled from the scene of the killing.

In its entire investigation the Commission has found no evidence of conspiracy, subversion, or disloyalty to the United States Government by any Federal, State, or local official. On the basis of the evidence before the Commission it concludes that Oswald acted alone.

Question No. 1: Which of the following is NOT evidence that Oswald acted alone in assassinating President Kennedy?

(A) There is no credible evidence that shots were fired from the Triple Underpass.

(B) Oswald attempted to kill Maj. Gen. Walker.

(C) A total of three shots were fired at Kennedy and Connally by a rifle from a 6th-floor window of the Texas School Book Depository.

(D) Oswald owned the rifle that fired the three shots fired at Kennedy and Connally.

(E) Oswald was present at the 6th-floor window at the Texas School Book Depository at the time of the assassination.

Question No. 2: Which of the following is the best evidence that the bullets that killed Kennedy were fired from the Texas School Book Depository?

(A) Three shots were fired.

(B) Oswald lied to the police after his arrest.

(C) The windshield of the limousine was hit but not shattered.

(D) The nature of Connally and Kennedy's bullet wounds and location of the car at the time of the shots establish they were fired from above and behind, placing their origin at the Texas Book Depository 6th floor.

(E) Oswald's rifle was found in the Texas School Book Depository.

Question No. 3: The significance of Oswald's attempt to kill Maj. Gen. Walker on April 10th, 1963 as to the Kennedy assassination was:

(A) His capability of killing another human being

(B) His hatred for authority

(C) His mental instability

(D) Evidence of conspiracy

(E) Walker's probable involvement in the assassination.

Question No. 4: Evidence that Oswald also killed Patrolman Tippitt was:

(A) The Magruder film

(B) Oswald's confession

(C) Eyewitness testimony

(D) DNA evidence

(E) Photographs.

Question No. 5: The Commission did NOT consider which of the following in its analysis of evidence?

(A) Eyewitness testimony.

(B) Ballistics evidence.

(C) Films of the assassination.

(D) Expert reports.

(E) Oswald's confession.

Question No. 6: The Commission believed Oswald acted alone because:

(A) Oswald lied after his arrest

(B) Oswald murdered Tippitt

(C) Expert reports proved no one else was involved

(D) No other person was seen in the assassination films

(E) No evidence was found of any other person involved.

Passage IX A

The notion of global warming is a myth, something dreamed up for reasons that politicians and doomsday sayers always have up their sleeve, I suppose. Ph.D.s in Climatology, such as Canadian professor, Dr. Timothy Ball, have tried in vain to explain that global warming is not a phenomenon even remotely caused by or contributed to by humans adding too much carbon dioxide, or anything else, to the earth's atmosphere. Dr. Ball has called the public hysterical rampage on global warming the "greatest deception in the history of science." One may as well argue the world is flat. What is actually occurring is that the earth is doing its own thing, as it has been doing for uncounted millennia, since before humans were here, and no doubt as it will long after humans have run their course, like the dinosaurs and other extinct species. The earth is emerging from a mini-ice age, which means it is naturally warming up. This is what the earth has always done in its cycles out of ice ages. This fact does not give humans license to flagrantly and stupidly pollute, destruct, and waste the resources particularly necessary for our species' survival. It does not excuse politicians from using a fact of nature of cosmic proportion to further their pork barrel agendas. Instead of funding useless studies to reverse something impossible to change, humanity should be examining itself and its own lifestyles to determine how it should be adapting to the inevitable changes evolving in the earth's environment. In other words, not how do we change the world to fit us, but how do we change us to fit the world? That is not how the politicians and big business want us to think, however, until it is economically in their best interests for us to do so.

Passage IX B

An international panel of distinguished scientists, including noted climatologists, have concluded "unequivocally" that global warming is a fact and that "we [humans] did it." Industrial pollution, car exhaust, paved earth, deforestation, rising levels of carbon dioxide, higher acid levels in the oceans and in the atmosphere, all have contributed. Projects indicate significant temperature rises and disappearance of the Arctic Sea ice by 2100. Existing deserts will expand significantly and new ones will arise. The effect on businesses, food sources, and potable water will be dramatic. Some experts believe there are opportunities to slow warming and at the same time allow for adaptation to the changing conditions. Suggestions for new key resources such as wind farms, solar energy, and other alternative fuel sources are important ways to reduce the deadly green house gas emissions that have caused this crisis.

Question No. 1: The one thing the writers of the Passages A and B seem to agree upon is:

(A) Humans are causing global warming

(B) Humans can stop global warming

(C) Dinosaurs started global warming

(D) We are entering an ice age

(E) The earth is experiencing global warming.

Question No. 2: Dr. Timothy Ball is an expert who states:

(A) Humanity should join worldwide to avert global warming

(B) There is nothing we can do to avert global warming

(C) The world is flat

(D) Global warming is caused by the Industrial Revolution

(E) A panel of experts is working on a plan to halt global warning.

Question No. 3: Writer of Passage B reports that global warming is caused by all EXCEPT which one of the following?

(A) Deforestation.

(B) Industrial pollution.

(C) Paved earth.

(D) Artificial lakes.

(E) Higher levels of carbon dioxide in the atmosphere.

Question No. 4: Both writers agree humanity should be able to:

(A) Adapt to the changes caused by global warming

(B) Stop global warming

(C) Learn from the dinosaurs

(D) Build wind farms

(E) Move to a new planet.

Question No. 5: The writer of Passage A holds the opinion that global warming is:

(A) A sociological problem

(B) A natural phenomenon being used by economic opportunists

(C) A valid source of grants for academic study of its causes

(D) A responsibility of government to be brought under control by 2010

(E) A subject for study by an international coalition of experts.

Question No. 6: The difference between writer A and writer B is best stated as which of the following:

(A) A relates the effects of the earth to humans while B relates the effects of humans to themselves

(B) A relates the effects of the universe to the earth while B relates the effects of humans to the earth.

(C) B relates the effects of humans to their environment while A relates the effects of the environment to humans

(D) A relates the effect of the earth to humans while B relates the effects of humans to the earth

(E) A relates the effects of the earth's natural cosmic evolution to the phenomenon of global warming while B relates the effects of human lifestyle to the phenomenon of global warming.

Passage X

Title VII of the federal Civil Rights Act prohibits a covered employer (one who employs 15 or more employees) from discriminating in hire or in other terms and conditions of employment on the basis of race, color, religion, gender, nationality, and other certain classifications. The human resources manager of a large company has four finalist candidates to consider for a middle management position. The requirements for the job will include out of town travel of several days per month; minimum bachelor's degree; computer skills in the company's choice of software programs; and satisfactory profiling on the employment testing all candidates take. Experience in the company's area of service is preferred but not required. The four candidates under review all possess at least the minimum qualifications (some more) for the skill sets the company is seeking and all four are comparable on the testing. It will now come down to a more subjective evaluation of the candidates in the final interview process. The interviewers are looking for someone who will be able to work well the company team, get on well with customers, indicate self-motivation, make a good initial presentation, and self confidence. In the interviews, which take place in a relaxed atmosphere over lunch, the human resources manager and an executive team representative of the company meet each candidate and learn the following information.

Passage X

1. Female candidate 1 has an MBA, is articulate and well-traveled in previous jobs. She mentioned without being asked that she is newly married, as an explanation of a recent name change on her resume. She interviews well.

2. Male candidate 2 has a BA, is quiet spoken. This is his first job interview out of college. He comes with a high GPA, excellent internship references and could be hired at the lower end of the salary range. He has no previous management experience, however.

3. Female candidate 3 has a BA and 5 years experience in a similar job with one of the company's competitors. The interviewers know not to ask about her marital status but quietly note she wears a wedding ring.

4. Female candidate 4 has a BA, and is halfway through a program toward an MBA plus 2 years experience in a similar field and job. She also wears a wedding ring.

The company hires male candidate number 2. Each of the three female candidates files charges of discrimination on the basis of gender with the Equal Employment Opportunity Commission (EEOC). The EEOC is the federal agency that investigates claims of discrimination in employment under Title VII. A woman claiming discrimination in hiring can state at least an initial case if she is passed over in favor of a man. The employer can rebut the claim by proving a legitimate neutral business reason for its hiring decision.

Question No 1: If the company discriminated, which of the following is a likely unstated unlawful assumption the company made about the female candidates with respect to the company's job requirements?

(A) Women do not work as hard as men.

(B) Men work harder than women.

(C) The female candidates were over qualified.

(D) These women are overachievers and will be troublemakers.

(E) Married women do not need the work as much as a man.

Question No. 2: The easiest way for the company to have avoided a discrimination claim would have been to:

(A) Hire female candidate no. 4

(B) Hire female candidate no. 1

(C) Hire female candidate no. 3

(D) Hire none of the candidates and start over

(E) Hire any one of the three female candidates.

Question No. 3: Assuming the female candidates charging discrimination can prove the company noted, and considered the women's marital status in its hiring decision, this point evidences discrimination because:

(A) The company did not note if the male candidate was married

(B) The company assumed a married woman was less job worthy than the male candidate

(C) The company did not consider female candidates' MBA

(D) the company did not consider the female candidates' work experience

(E) the company hired the only male candidate.

Question No. 4: Which of the following facts, if true, would best help the company refute the discrimination claim?

(A) Each of the female candidates revealed in her interview that she would not accept a minimum salary within the company's salary range for the position.

(B) The male candidate was not married.

(C) The male candidate was also married.

(D) Each of the female candidates volunteered in her interview she was planning to get pregnant as soon as possible.

(E) Each of the female candidates volunteered in her interview that she was pregnant.

Question No. 5: The women's best evidence that the company discriminated by hiring the male candidate is:

(A) He is male

(B) They are married

(C) He is cheaper

(D) He is less qualified and least experienced than any of the women

(E) He is better qualified than most of the women.

Question No. 6: Which of the following, if true, would assist the company in refuting the charge of discrimination?

(A) The male candidate was hired because he is the nephew of the company's CEO.

(B) The Management team leader does not like working with women.

(C) The previous person in that job was a woman and had filed a sexual harassment complaint.

(D) The Management team leader was concerned the women would get pregnant and present problems with the travel component of the job.

(E) None of the above; nothing will help the company with this one.

Answers

Passage I

1. (D) 2. (C) 3. (D) 4. (C) 5. (B) 6. (E)

Passage II

1. (C) 2. (A) 3. (E) 4. (A) 5. (B) 6. (C)

PASSAGE III

1. (A) 2. (C) 3. (E) 4. (D) 5. (B) 6. (A)

Passage IV

1. (C) 2. (E) 3. (A) 4. (D) 5. (A) 6. (C)

Passage V

1. (C) 2. (D) 3. (D) 4. (C) 5. (D) 6. (C)

Passage VI

1. (A) 2. (E) 3. (B) 4. (E) 5. (C) 6. (E)

Passage VII

1. (C) 2. (A) 3. (C) 4. (D) 5. (B) 6. (A)

Passage VIII

1. (B) 2. (D) 3. (A) 4. (C) 5. (E) 6. (E)

Passage IX

1.(E) 2. (B) 3. (D) 4. (A) 5. (B) 6. (E)

Passage X

1. (E) 2. (E) 3. (A) 4. (A) 5. (D) 6. (A)

6

The Writing Sample

98. Basis for the Writing Sample

The writing exercise of the LSAT is set up to be completed in 35 minutes. You will be given a lined page to write your essay. Your response is not scored, but it is sent to the law schools to which you have applied, and any one of them may use it to assess your writing skills as part of the admission process. Opinions differ on the importance of the writing sample. The Writing Sample could well be the deciding factor when applicants are otherwise closely qualified. If you and the Internet know about professional services for the law school application's personal statement, so do the law schools. The Writing Sample of the LSAT is something you have to write without anyone's assistance. Thus, while the writing sample does not affect your LSAT numerical score, it is a part of the LSAT and may be influential in the admissions process.

The writing sample commonly presents a decision or argument based on specific facts. The test question will provide directions about the topic to be addressed. The question commonly presents two positions, and asks you to make a choice between them and defend your choice. A decision question for your essay might look like the following which is a hypothetical that is similar to questions utilized on past LSATs:

"James Smith is a physical therapist who wants to set up a new business selling custom-designed exercise and physical therapy equipment. Part of his service is individual assessment of his buyer's needs, and providing equipment for an individualized program. James wants to select the best location that is both affordable and likely to be a place attractive to potential customers. He has found two potential locations.

The first property is a storefront with a deep narrow space. It is located between a Starbucks coffee shop and a discount men's wear store in a busy shopping center that has a fair amount of parking, and a bus stop at its corner. This property requires a two-year lease commitment. It is available for immediate occupancy and could use a coat of paint.

The second property offers almost twice the floor space of the first one, and is located in a newer area being developed outside of town. It also is available for immediate occupancy and is move-in ready. The rent is $200 a month more than the first property but the landlord only requires a one-year lease. So far the only other space occupied in this new area is a children's day care center. The landlord advises James that there will be at least four other tenants within the next six months, one of which may be a doctor's office, although that lease has not yet been signed. There is ample parking, but no public transport. Construction is still underway in some of the units.

Which property is better for James' start-up business?

99. Organization of the Writing Sample Answer

This Writing Sample challenges you to take a side and persuade the reader why the decision you have chosen is better. There is no right or wrong answer. Consider what James' goal is for his business, and the type of business. The approach is to first identify the pros and cons of each property. List them on scratch paper that the test will provide you. What are the factors relevant to making the decision — location, type of traffic, public access, cost, term of lease, space, type of business? Your notes might look like this:

Location	Pros	Cons
In town storefront	Public Transport Established traffic brought in by other stores Cheaper monthly lease Ample Parking	Other stores very different from his type of business 2-year commitment Needs some rehab Smaller of the two locations by half Retail area — different from his type of business
New building	1-year lease commitment Ample parking Move-in ready Twice the floor space Up and coming area Landlord appears to be seeking professional services and similar business — childcare and physician office — physician referral source	Outside of town No public transport Only one other business in operation Physician office lease not yet locked-in Higher rent by $200/month Risk the area will not develop as hoped

The established area will have more traffic, but will it be the kind of traffic he needs? You should evaluate the type of clientele you believe the Starbucks and men's wear store will bring past James' door. In contrast, being in a larger-sized store near a physician's office that could be a potential referral source is attractive — except whether the physician's office will materialize is a risk. On the other hand, it does indicate the type of businesses the developer is soliciting for the newer location. One property costs more, but is the cost mitigated by only a one-year lease commitment? The established location also has current public transportation. The new office does not. Is that a relevant factor for James' decision making? You should not add facts outside the problem presented, but you can make some logical inferences in reaching your decision.

Having made a decision as to which location you would recommend, organize your answer with a quick outline before starting to write your essay on the test paper. In law school, you characteristically will outline cases and organize essays according to the IRAC approach: Issue, Rule, Analysis (applying the rule to the facts), Conclusion. This approach provides a logical analogy for organizing your response in the Writing Sample. Considering the pros and cons, quickly make a decision and mark the items on your notes that support your decision. Jot down an outline to organize your essay.

Begin your answer with a statement summarizing the problem. You do not have a legal rule to apply in this hypothetical essay, but you can state in place of that concept that James needs to choose the best location to establish and grow a new business, noting that customers and cost are the two key elements. State your decision briefly, such as, "The xx location is James' best choice because……." In a new paragraph, identify the pros and cons of each place and explain which of those outweighs the other to support your conclusion, which you will restate at the end: "For these reasons, James' best choice is xx."

If a law school evaluates your writing sample, it is going to look for organization, succinct and correct use of language (including the niceties of punctuation, tense, diction, spelling and grammar), and clarity of reasoning in support of your decision. It is not so much what you decide but how you present your decision. This essay question could be argued either way as both locations have "pros" and "cons."

An important key to presenting your response to the Writing Sample question is to stay on topic and stick to the facts stated in the problem. If you elect to write about something unrelated or bring in facts that are not part of the problem presented, you will have wasted your effort and nullified your response. Also, writing about something else entirely is worse than leaving it blank. If you address the topic squarely and clearly, write in sentences with words you can spell, and write legibly, you will fare well in an admissions officer's review of your Writing Sample. An essay responding to the above Writing Sample question might look like the following:

James is starting a new business with no established client base. His business is a combination of providing customized product (exercise/physical therapy equipment), and a service, in the form of his expertise, as a physical therapist to advise his clientele in the type and use of his equipment. He needs a location amenable to his type of clientele at a rate he can afford. It is reasonable to assume that his principle customers will be two types of people: those who have disposable income to spend to enhance their physical health and those who have medical conditions or physical limitations that require a guided rehabilitation program. James has a choice of the retail storefront in the established center or the newly constructed space outside of town that is still under development. For the following reasons I advise James to choose the new development option.

1. **Lease commitment and cost:** Although the newly-built space costs $200/month more than the storefront space, it requires only a 1-year commitment as opposed to the 2-year lease required for the storefront. James is starting a new business with all the economic risks inherent in a new business venture. If he is not able to sustain his new business in the storefront option, he will be locked into a two-year commitment that he may not be able to pay. The 2-year commitment is likely to be a higher financial commitment, overall, than the more expensive one-year lease. James is getting double the space for only $200 more; a sum that is likely less than double the storefront rent. Another cost factor in favor of the newer space is that it is move-in ready — the other location is not.

2. **Size of space:** The newly built location is twice the size of the older storefront. Because James needs to showcase various types of equipment and demonstrate its use on site, he will be able to make a better presentation in the new space; the storefront space is smaller and more narrow.

3. **Location:** While the storefront may have more established traffic at this point in time, the newer location is up and coming. People are likely to be more attracted to the newer, fresher location and respond positively to the

feeling of spaciousness. Although it is not yet established and therefore a risk, the proposed proximity of a doctor's office to the new space raises the opportunity for referrals to James' business because he is convenient for the doctor and the patients. The new location clearly is geared toward professional service establishments as evidenced by the day care center and the landlord's expectation of acquiring a doctor's office. James' type of business fits this demographic better than the retail establishments: coffee shop and men's wear store.

4. **Parking and accessibility:** Both spaces offer sufficient parking. The new development does not have public transportation service at this time, but it is reasonable to expect that most of James' potential clientele will be people who have the means to provide their own transportation. His service is not one where the same people will be visiting frequently. They will come for a product and instruction, requiring two visits at most. Further, the absence of public transportation is offset by the other values provided by the newly-built space.

For these reasons I recommend the new location outside of town as James' best choice for launching his new business.

7

Test Day

100. Prepare for the Test

If there is one word that summarizes this entire book, that word is "preparation." The point applies no less to the day of the test. At the time of this book's publication, the following describes the LSAT Test Day. Be aware that LSAC can, and has, changed its rules and requirements from time to time. Always obtain up-to-the-minute information for the registration process and Test Day procedures.

LSAC offers registration options online, by mail, or by phone; information is available at **www.lsac.org**. It is recommended that an applicant to most law schools sit for the LSAT no later than December in the year preceding expected law school matriculation. LSAC schedules the test at various locations nationwide, more often than not on Saturdays, but also on other dates to accommodate Saturday Sabbath observers. If you have any physical accessibility requirements, resolve those with LSAC ahead of time.

Eat breakfast whether you want to or not; you need brain food for the LSAT. If you are a coffee person, do not skip it; this is not the day to decide to quit drinking coffee, but do not overdo it either. If you are not a morning person and cannot face a meal when you get up, you should take that into account, and get going early enough to be past your morning funk so you can have a brain empowering meal before it is time to leave for the test. Choose a healthy breakfast that will stay with you. High carbohydrates and empty sugars, like doughnuts and tasty cinnamon rolls, will bring a mental crash an hour after consumption.

LSAC advises to expect Test Day to consume seven hours. Plan for Test Day in a way to minimize as much stress on yourself as possible; it is worth stating what should be obvious. Get a good night's sleep, and be sure you are guaranteed to get up and going in plenty of time; alarm clock, friend, whatever it takes. Know where the test is being held, how to get there, how long it will take to get there, where to park, and how much it costs to park. LSAC warns that you are not permitted to bring anything to the test except your Admissions Ticket, photo identification, analog watch, and pencils. You should have several No. 2 pencils (HB for Canadian test locations), sharpened, with workable, easy, non-smear erasers. LSAC does not provide pencil sharpeners and does not permit mechanical pencils.

101. What You Can and Cannot Take into the Test

All your preparation will be for naught, and so will your score, if you are not prepared for Test Day's restrictions. There are several things that LSAC absolutely prohibits at the test site including during the break. As of the writing of this book, these are "books, papers of any kind, backpacks, handbags, earplugs, mechanical pencils, rulers, calculators, timers of any kind (except analog wristwatches), cellular phones, recording or photographic devices, pagers, beepers, headsets, or other electronic devices." LSAC further warns that "Bringing prohibited items into the test room may result in the confiscation of such items by the test supervisor, a warning, dismissal from the test center, or cancellation of a test score by LSAC. Prohibited items may not be used during the break. LSAC and LSAT testing staff are not responsible for candidates' belongings."

The items you are permitted to bring include: pencils, highlighter (to help you in marking items in the test booklet if you so desire), a drink (maximum 20 ounce size), a snack, Admissions Ticket, photo ID, tissues, medicine, keys and wallet. They must be contained in a clear plastic, ziplock bag (maximum one gallon size) that you will keep under your chair during the test. Drinks, medicines, and snacks will be permitted only at the break. Of the items you are permitted to bring in the plastic bag, only the following will be allowed on the desktop during the test: tissues, photo ID, wooden pencils, erasers, pencil sharpener, highlighter, and analog wristwatch.

Dress in comfortable clothes in layers because it could be a cold or hot room, a room that starts out cold and gets much warmer over the time you are in it, or vice versa. Except for religious apparel, LSAC does not permit test takers to wear hoods or hats. If you have a question about your apparel for religious reasons, it is advisable to check with LSAC about it before Test Day.

LSAC issues an Admissions Ticket in advance — when you register for the test. Do not leave home without it. The Admissions Ticket evidences your right to sit for the test and contains the test's exact date and reporting time, test site address, test center instructions, and test center procedures. LSAC publishes the test registration dates online, including late registration dates and times by mail, online and by telephone. If you registered online you should have printed your Admissions Ticket at that time. If you lose it you can reprint it off the LSAC Web site. Otherwise you will need to call LSAC by telephone about a lost Admissions Ticket. LSAC recommends that you check your LSAT online account the night before the test because there could be a change in reporting address. If there is a change, you will need to print out the revised Admissions Ticket.

Along with the Admissions Ticket the testing center proctor will require you to present a form of current (not expired) government-issued photo identification. Your first and last name on your identification must match the first and last name on your Admissions Ticket. Identification issues must be resolved with LSAC prior to Test Day by contacting LSAC through e-mail at **LSACINFO@LSAC.org** or by telephone at 215.968.1001. Identification may be re-checked at any time during the test.

Once the test begins, no one will be admitted. If you are late, you will miss the test. The test administrators will assign seats, and confiscate any items you have brought that are not permitted. As part of the identification procedure you will provide a thumbprint, and sign a statement that you are the person registered to take the test. The test administrator will distribute the test booklets and answer sheets, and call start and stop for each test section. A 10 to 15 minute break will be called after Section III.

To summarize, here is a Test Day Checklist. Leave everything else at home or locked in your car:

- LSAC Admissions Ticket — Checked online the night before

- Current Photo ID e.g., Driver's License, Passport, Military ID

- No. 2 or HB wooden pencils (At least three or four) with good erasers; option — separate eraser for clean erasure of pencil on answer sheet.

- Analog wristwatch — not digital.

- Directions to your test location and parking.

- Your own pencil sharpener.

- Highlighter.

- Drink in plastic bottle or drink box — Max. 20 oz./491 ml.

- Snack.

- Tissues.

- Medication or other medical products.

- Keys and wallet.

- All of the above in no larger than a one gallon clear plastic Ziplock bag.

8

On a Lighter Note

There have been some lighthearted studies of people's superstitions for good luck on test days, game days, airplanes, and lottery purchases. Around 80 percent of people surveyed possess some kind of private token or ritual to help them on an exam. All kinds of things come into play from lucky socks to lucky shirts, medals, recitations, rituals, and jewelry. These beliefs range from fun tokenism to deep seated or even compulsive needs. While it is not likely that your choice of wardrobe can substitute for good advance LSAT test preparation, this writer would be the last to discourage you from any harmless extra that you believe will bolster your confidence. If you have a pair of lucky socks, by all means, wear them on Test Day.

Case Studies

Case Study: Virtual LSAT Proctor

Virtual LSAT Proctor

SELF Proctor

PO Box 181, Allenwood, NJ 08720

www.lsatproctor.com

(732) 996-7599 - voice

support@lsatproctor.com

Founders: Mike Wilkos, Patrick Rogers

I (Mike Wilkos) was surprised at how intimidating the LSAT examination environment was, and how it can so greatly impact your score. Losing concentration in the middle of a Reading Comprehension passage because the test taker next to you cannot stop coughing or blowing his nose is a very possible reality. Having the proctor strictly enforce the "pencils down" announcement was also a real eye opener. As a test taker, you need to be prepared for the distracting LSAT environment because, unfortunately, things outside of your control can affect your score.

Case Study: Virtual LSAT Proctor

This not only has been my first-hand experience, but also has been the reason stated by very many test takers for why they, too, scored significantly lower on the real LSAT examinations compared to their advance practice exams. They were caught off guard by the almost non-existent breaks between test sections, strict enforcement of timing, and the distracting variables and elements of taking the exam in a public setting.

These demands of the LSAT proved to me there was no valid shortcut to preparation. The ideal person that would receive a high score on the LSAT would begin studying six months in advance. This person would be well organized in study habits so that she or he would avoid getting overwhelmed by the rigorous material. This person would complete the full-length actual LSAT practice exams under the actual LSAT conditions—strict test day timing and distractions. By doing so, the test taker will feel better prepared and reduce the level of anxiety come test day. Also, this person would spend time scrutinizing wrongs answers in order to better understand the method to which the right answers can be obtained.

Although a six-month preparation period is ideal, this will vary for each individual because different people have different capabilities in studying and understanding the standardized test material. But since the LSAT is such a rigorous and intense examination, we feel that getting to know the material six months prior to the test allows for a successful balance of study time with work and social life. Otherwise, preparing too late may cause frequent cramming sessions, and may overwhelm test takers. On the other hand, studying more than six months prior to test day may leave the person disillusioned with the test. Preparing so far in advance may leave the test taker "burned out," and may not lead to any additional benefit. Also, by the time of

Case Study: Virtual LSAT Proctor

the test the test taker may have scaled back some of his or her study habits. We feel that steadily increasing one's LSAT focus over a six month period until a week or so before the test is the best preparation method. In this way, the test taker will have the proper strategies and techniques fresh in their head with a minimal amount of test anxiety.

The most challenging portions of the LSAT will depend upon on the individual's strengths and weaknesses. We find that people may sometimes be more adept at Logic Games but struggle with Reading Comprehension. Or, they may be better at Reading Comprehension but have trouble with Logical Reasoning. Several factors such as educational background, right/left brain dominance, visual-spatial intelligence, and speed reading ability also play into a person's strengths and weaknesses for the respective sections of the LSAT.

However, all takers of the LSAT face the same constraints of time, focus, and distraction. The idea for the Virtual LSAT Proctor actually arose out of necessity when I realized that my true ability was not reflected in my first LSAT score because I was not used to taking the test in a distracting public environment. On my first LSAT administration, I received a score that was lower than what I was both aiming for and practicing at. Over the summer between my first and second LSAT administrations, we created the Virtual LSAT Proctor and were confident that we could help other test takers solve the problems that I had experienced during my first LSAT administration. I used the Virtual LSAT Proctor to prepare for my next LSAT administration, and I achieved a score ten points higher than my first score!

The main goal of the Virtual LSAT Proctor is to help test takers become more comfortable with the strict test day timing and procedures of the LSAT while helping them become desensitized to the distractions present in their testing environment.

Case Study: Virtual LSAT Proctor

The pressure of the time limits imposed by the LSAT can be overcome by taking and retaking full length practice exams under real LSAT conditions. In fact, it is crucial to simulate actual LSAT conditions as much as possible. If you do not do so, you are going to lack endurance, speed, and confidence on test day. You will be unprepared in ways you had not anticipated. This will cause anxiety during the test, which can lead to panicking, loss of concentration, and ultimately, a lower score.

However, it can be hard to strictly and accurately time one's self when studying alone. Furthermore, the use of digital timers has been banned since the June 2007 test, and only analog watches are permitted. This makes it even more difficult to adhere to the strict time limits of the LSAT. Virtual LSAT Proctor has been designed to enable you to simulate realistic LSAT administrations to assist you with strictly timing yourself, and the "built-in distractions" feature will allow you to become desensitized to any concentration-breaking distractions in the testing environment.

Loss of time from distraction is the exact problem that the Virtual LSAT Proctor is meant to solve. Being able to have an independent timer for your LSAT practice tests is vital. With the amount of studying a person does in preparation for the LSAT, it is common for test takers to want to give up or not be as rigorous with their preparation habits. In fact, many test takers "cheat" during practice tests by taking breaks in between sections and continuing to work after time has expired. But if you are not disciplined in adhering to the strict LSAT regulations, then you will face the unpleasant reality of a lower score on test day.

With the Virtual LSAT Proctor, test takers simply press the play button once and they instantly have access to a realistic LSAT testing environment and test proctor that will keep them focused, disciplined, and motivated, and thus achieve a higher score.

Case Study: Jay A. Cutts

Jay A. Cutts

Cutts Graduate Reviews

(800) 353-4898

Email: cutts@cuttsreviews.com

www.cuttsreviews.com

I'd like to introduce you to Annie, a typical prelaw student wrestling with the LSAT. Annie has always worked hard and gotten pretty decent grades, but her practice LSAT scores are just embarrassing. In fact, she is starting to wonder if she should forget about law school.

Why is Annie, a perfectly smart and capable student, having so much trouble when her roommate, who walked into the test without studying, got a 175? The answer has to do with processing style; the particular kind of thinking strategies that you use most effectively to solve problems. There is one particular thinking style that works best on the LSAT. People with that style can do well almost automatically. People whose strengths lie in other styles may have trouble. The good news, though, is that most people can learn to use the thinking style that the test requires.

Let's watch what happens as Annie begins to master the test. Annie has started prepping eight months before her planned October test. She knows she is going to need some help, and has compared her prep options. She has decided to work with a prep specialist who has many years experience, and who can work with her individually. The first thing Annie learns about is timing strategy. In her first test practice test she gives herself about a minute on each question and is able to get through the whole section. However, almost half the questions she worked on were wrong. Her first lesson asks her to start questioning her strategy and suggests new ways to use her time that will get her

Case Study: Jay A. Cutts

more points even if she does not finish the section. If she sticks with this and gets regular feedback from her prep specialist, she will eventually have complete control over the use of her time during the test, and will find that there is no longer a feeling of time pressure.

Did I mention that Annie suffers from serious test anxiety? It is bad enough that her entire life depends on the results of this test, but she has a long running history of just getting upset, feeling miserable and messing up on standardized tests. Once she has mastered timing strategy, she will be happily surprised to find that most of the anxiety is gone. This is because a lot of test anxiety centers around being caught between wanting to go faster to get to more questions, and needing to go slower to be more accurate, and no matter which one you do you're sure you did the wrong thing. When you have worked out in advance, exactly how to use your time for maximum points, there is nothing to be anxious about on the Test Day.

The other aspect of test anxiety is the feeling that you simply do not think the way the test writers think. You pick a perfectly good answer for perfectly good reasons, and then find out your answer is wrong. You might be able to see that their answer can be right but it is often impossible to see why it is any better than yours. Annie runs into this constantly and complains to her prep specialist that she is always getting down to two answers and picking the wrong one. How is she supposed to know which one the test writers like better? It just seems like an arbitrary judgment call.

Annie has actually stumbled on the heart of mastering the LSAT, although she does not know it yet. In her next lesson she will learn that it is never that one answer is better than another. Of the two answers she is considering, one of them is dead wrong. It has a fatal flaw in it. The other answer is indisputably correct. And the LSAT people can

Case Study: Jay A. Cutts

prove that their answer is right, and the other one wrong in court, if necessary. Feel like suing them?

Most of Annie's study over the next few months will consist of learning in more detail the hundreds, and perhaps thousands, of patterns that the LSAT uses to create fatal flaws and to defend correct answers. She will also learn strategies for working two answers against each other, so that instead of getting frustrated and just guessing, she will be able to turn that energy into focused analysis.

Annie will learn that while the patterns are similar throughout all sections of the test, there are some specific strategies she can use for each type of section. In Reading Comprehension she will learn strategies for quickly organizing the passage and for avoiding careless errors. For Logical Reasoning she will learn to recognize several common types of logical argument, and how to dissect if/then logic. In the Analytical Reasoning she will learn how to avoid common pitfalls in setting up the passage, in misunderstanding the question stems, and in trying to create diagrams. Then she will learn an extremely systematic approach to solving the games so that she does not go in circles.

Because Annie is trying to learn the hidden patterns built into the test, she practices only with actual LSAT questions published by Law Services. She found that many of the simulated questions in commercial prep books did not accurately represent LSAT patterns, according to her prep specialist. In fact, his suggestion is that the only practice materials she needs are the Law Services tests, in addition, of course, to his lectures and handouts!

Annie has been practicing about seven to ten hours a week now for a few months, and is trying to apply the strategies she has learned. While she is making some headway on her own, she finds that her

Case Study: Jay A. Cutts

one-on-one work with her prep specialist helps her see patterns and learn new strategies that she was not learning on her own, and to do so more quickly. In the first month or two it seemed to her that almost every question had a new pattern but now she is recognizing many patterns and there are fewer that still throw her for a loop. When she finds one, she goes over it with her prep specialist and he can quickly help her understand it. And guess what; the next day she finds that new pattern on another test — and gets it right.

If Annie continues this way for the next few months — working with her prep specialist on both new patterns and on timing strategy — she cannot help but be at her best for the October test. However, she is not going to put all of her eggs in the LSAT basket. She is also starting to work on her Personal Statement, the next most important part of her law school application. Fortunately, her prep specialist is also an expert in other areas of the admissions process, and helps her understand the difference between the right and wrong ways to stand out from the crowd.

I bet you would like to know what is going to happen to Annie. Having made her up, I can tell you with some confidence that she will go into the October test feeling rather nervous but will find that once the test starts, she knows exactly what to do. She will know approximately how she is going to score, because she has taken a number of practice tests in the last week. She will get a strong score that she is proud of but it will not be high enough to absolutely guarantee her a place at her top choice school. Having worked hard on her Personal Statement and the rest of her application, she will look like a strong candidate when the admissions committee reviews her file. Will they take her? Will she have to go to her second choice school? Like Annie, we will just have to wait these long months to find out. But I can tell you that,

Case Study: Jay A. Cutts

whatever happens, Annie is now prepared to make the best of it, and if necessary, to do whatever it takes to make sure she will get into a school she is proud to attend.

Case Study: Makalika Naholowa'a

Makalika Naholowa'a

Law Student

Columbia University School of Law

Without question, advance preparation for the LSAT is important. But it needs to be the right type of preparation. I am living proof that you can significantly improve your LSAT score. My first diagnostic score was 163, and by Test Day I was able to earn a 179.

There's no real limit on how dramatic your improvement can be, although some testing services state that a certain range of increase (maybe only 6 or 8 points) are normal. You must ignore those statistics, shake it off, and just go for it. There are several professional LSAT assistants on the market. I think Kaplan LSAT 180 is good. There are also individual tutors and books available.

In deciding what you are going to need for your preparation for the LSAT, I recommend taking a practice test as soon as you know that you are possibly interested in the law school admissions process. How you field the first practice test will give you a sense for how far you need to go. My personal hunch is that students can learn to get near to a 180 LSAT score by adopting effective study strategies and not limiting themselves to a prescribed amount of time that worked

Case Study: Makalika Naholowa'a

for someone else. Some people will take longer than others to reach optimal readiness, and although there is an interest in keeping a nice spread of scores for applying the curve which I think translates into encouraging students to prepare, but "not too much," there is technically no limit on how long you can spend preparing. LSAT prep is as custom a program as any other general study habits. Some strategies are generally recommended and those can be useful as guidelines. However, each person has different techniques that work for him or her, and those techniques may be less effective for other people. What worked for me was to make LSAT prep a part of my normal every day life, so that the questions and thought processes they require would become second nature. For example, I would work on practice sections in the car (when my husband was driving) or at lunch, or just whenever I had a moment. But I tried to do them daily to boost retention and familiarity.

When asked which sections of the LSAT tend to be the most challenging to people, I answer, "all of it." The level of challenge will vary with individual skill sets. Reading Comprehension hurts slow readers and those intimidated by topics that feel foreign to them, particularly those focused on science topics. Arguments tend to frustrate those who are not detail-oriented and have not been taught what the key words are in a typical question of this type, and what their meanings are. Games probably have the highest scare value, but yet seem to be the easiest to crack with competent instruction on how to identify applicable diagramming schemes.

One comfort I can offer about preparing for the LSAT is that it is predictable. Each LSAT may be a "new" version, but it will not be original. It follows a formula. Learn the formula and you will do well on your test. Through diligent use of the practice tests and the market array of preparatory materials, you can become acquainted with the

Case Study: Makalika Naholowa'a

test sections and the approach within each section. They recycle the same old tricks into every test, so if you practice enough of them, and really understand your practice exams, you should be fine on test day.

To improve your speed on the test, practice, practice, practice. Practice until you start to see patterns that allow you to plow through the content faster with higher accuracy. Nothing relieves pressure like confidence with the materials, and early successes. As you work through your practice questions, study the reasons why an answer choice is not credited. It is only through inspection on why something is wrong, as well as why the "correct" answer is right, that you will start to see gains. Also, remember that there are a great many more wrong answer choices than correct ones. Therefore, if, as you go through practice questions, you only focus on the why and wherefore of the "correct" answer, you will be ignoring a large portion of any question — that is why the wrong choices are not correct! The ability to identify those that are definitely wrong will sometimes allow you to eliminate all but the right, even if, otherwise, you would be unsure about that right response.

Because it is important to understand the relationship of all the answers to a practice test question, be sure that you utilize the preparatory test materials that give you detailed explanations. If your practice book does not provide the reasoning for why answers are credited and why the other choices are not credited, then the material is of no real use to you. You must review the wrong choices as well as the right ones to make progress toward a higher score. If you are plowing through practice questions, but not figuring out why you are getting the wrong answers (as well as the right ones), you may not be learning what you need for Test Day. If you find yourself doing this, you need to revise your prep approach and your choice of materials.

Case Study: Makalika Naholowa'a

I found the Games questions to be particularly challenging. I think most people do. A tip for decoding these questions is diagramming. Game diagramming can be difficult to acquire solely from a book. Individual tutoring is especially useful to learn diagramming. If you choose to take a class, make sure diagramming instruction is included. Interacting in person with a tutor or in a class will make it much easier. Who is the successful LSAT scorer? It is someone capable of pushing through test day anxiety; someone who is confident that s/he is going to do well; someone able to quickly rebound from troublesome sections and aggressively finish any remaining sections (even if a guess is required); someone who has prepared enough to have a comfort with the materials and pacing of the LSAT.

You cannot simulate how nervous you will actually be on Test Day. You can work in worst case scenario environments to prepare as best as you can. This means, work at a cramped desk, around lots of noise, maybe even a public place. Testing conditions are almost never ideal, so if you make sure that you are able to deal with all of the little inconveniences that Test Day facilities may throw at you, you will be in a good place.

Ultimately, try to think of the LSAT as a game. Most people like games, and future attorneys should enjoy a challenge. If you can separate the stakes from the exercise, it can actually be a somewhat enjoyable game to play. I know, that sounds unlikely! But my advice as one who has "been there" is: just give it a try!

Case Study: Ann K. Levine, Esq

Ann K. Levine, Esq.

Law School Admission Consultant

LawSchoolExpert.com

http://lawschoolexpert.blogspot.com

1-877-LAW-SKOL

As a former admissions director for two ABA-accredited law schools, I understand what it takes to get into law school. During my tenure in the admissions world, I realized that many students lacked direction about selecting law schools and putting together the best application package to showcase their abilities as future lawyers. Preparing for the LSAT is but one of several components of law school application, but certainly the LSAT is a significant factor.

A universal truth about the LSAT (or any achievement test like it) is that everyone wants a higher score. Wanting it is not the point of the exercise. The LSAT is an aptitude test. If you put everything into the test that you have available – your time and resources and effort - then the idea is to get a score that shows your aptitude for performance on that exam.

That is not to say a person cannot improve her score. Preparation and motivation are the keys. I had a client who started with an LSAT score of 157 without much preparation. He then dedicated himself to studying to take it a second time, and he raised his score to a 164. Still, he felt his practice exams scores in the low 170s were a better indication of his abilities and that he had bubbled answers incorrectly when he took the second LSAT. Determined to prove it, he took the test again and indeed scored a 173. This is not at all typical (taking the test three times and improving by such a great margin), but he was an

Case Study: Ann K. Levine, Esq

applicant who was trying to overcome unimpressive grades, so he was especially motivated. His is a case that proves preparation and determination can be a powerful combination to achieve a higher LSAT score.

If you did not do as well as you hoped on the LSAT, perform an honest assessment of yourself and your circumstances. Were your expectations reasonable? Are there study habits you can change and/or improve upon? Did something happen on Test Day that impacted your performance? Will you benefit from professional assistance? What is your history with standardized exams? Use the answers to these questions to adjust your strategy in preparing to re-take the exam.

There is no one cookie-cutter approach that will guarantee success – whatever score defines your measure of success. I work with my clients on an individual basis. It is important that you know yourself and how you learn. In devising your preparation plan, pick a timeline that has led you to succeed in the past and adjust it to your LSAT prep plan. If you know that you catch on to standardized tests quickly, then two months may be sufficient. If you typically struggle with these things, take more time and go at your own pace. However, never take the LSAT completely cold; this is not a test you will master by accident. Following a timeline given by a preparatory company may be helpful for those who know they need structure imposed upon them. The core of your preparation should be the practice tests. There is just no worthwhile substitute to using the past LSATs.

I do think there is such a thing as over-emphasizing LSAT preparation, which will lead to "over preparation" or burn-out before you ever get to the actual test. If, after studying for two to three months, your practice scores hit a plateau, there is no reason to postpone taking the LSAT in hopes of improving your score.

Case Study: Ann K. Levine, Esq

Most of my clients have the greatest trouble with the Logic Games, because they present a different way of thinking than generally required in the disciplines of political science, literature, and humanities, which are the prevalent undergraduate prelaw majors. The other component that can be a psychological barrier is the time limit of each LSAT section. The best way to approach the time factor is to understand that it is simply part of the test and not an obstacle to your success; everyone would do better on the LSAT if there were no time limits. In addition, no simulation will be able to duplicate what happens on Test Day because you cannot realistically simulate your nervousness on Test Day. Proctors and others are often distracting to people.

Many of my clients ask me how much time they should spend preparing for the Writing Sample portion of the LSAT. While it will not be scrutinized too heavily for English majors with good GPAs, the Writing Sample is especially important for students for whom English is a second language. Schools may use your LSAT Writing Sample essay to evaluate your true writing ability if they suspect you had significant assistance with the personal statement portion of the law school application. If this might be an issue for you, take a writing class and get help with this. Writing ability is something that cannot be corrected in a few weeks of study, but it is something you will need to conquer before starting law school, so you might as well be proactive and provide a creditable start with the Writing Sample portion of the LSAT.

Finally, put the LSAT in perspective. It is not an intelligence test. Your score is not a number forever stamped on your forehead by which you will be judged for the rest of your life. Do your best, and use the result to craft a strategy for your admission to law school. I help people through this process every day. Remember, even with a 180 and 3.9, admission is not guaranteed to any law school – schools take

Case Study: Ann K. Levine, Esq

outstanding applicants with numbers lower than their medians and 25th percentiles. The key is using the rest of the law school application to show what makes you an outstanding prospect for a future in law.

Case Study: Kelly Means, Esq

Kelly Means, Esq.

Fringe Benefits Section

Wickens, Herzer, Panza, Cook & Batista Co.

35765 Chester Road

Avon, OH 44011

(440) 930-8000

kmeans@wickenslaw.com

www.wickenslaw.com

As a recent law school graduate, I find looking back beyond the Bar Examination to the LSAT is a bit like double vision. Both are a challenge and I am proud both are successfully achieved. For the LSAT I found that most of my peers and I found the Logical Reasoning sections to be the most challenging, not so much because of their difficulty but because of the time constraints to get through them.

Time is the critical factor to overcome and the practice tests are very helpful for that. Going through the practice questions is the best way to become faster at the test questions and improve upon test-taking skills. I definitely recommend taking a course such as Kaplan as well as extra practice tests on your own time. I took Kaplan in the spring and sat for the LSAT in June. I found it an ideal time in which to prepare for the test. I recommend a course like Kaplan. Their course was conducted over 10 sessions of 3.5 hours each, and I practiced

Case Study: Kelly Means, Esq

tests in simulated conditions on my own time. This approach worked well for me. I liked the classroom course because it imposes the focus necessary to study efficiently.

I do believe it is possible for someone to "over prepare" for the LSAT by taking it to the point of becoming overly anxious. If you feel too stressed, that would be a sign that is what is happening. Maintaining a sense of calmness during the test is half the battle.

I did not find anything surprising on the LSAT. I believe this was because I took the time to thoroughly prepare with the assistance of experts in my preparation plan. It is by no means an easy test, but you can de-mystify it by understanding it for what it is.

Case Study: Kathy Daly, Esq

Kathy Daly, Esq.

Defense Litigation

Rupp, Baase, Pfalzgraf,

Cunningham & Coppola, LLC

1600 Liberty Building

Buffalo, NY 14202

My decision to go to Law School was both long anticipated and sudden. It was long anticipated because I had considered the option for many years. With every life change, the idea of applying to law school would cross my mind yet be dismissed as impractical for my current life circumstances. Looking back now, it would have been much easier to apply to law school then, when the seemingly difficult life circumstances only included a new boyfriend, change in employment, or moving to a new apartment.

Case Study: Kathy Daly, Esq

Eventually, I settled into a position as a psychiatric charge nurse at a local hospital. I met and married a nice man, had two children within 11 months of each other, bought a house, and a new show horse to promote across the country. Whatever possessed me to decide to apply to law school at that point in life is still a mystery. I tend to blame it on postpartum hormone changes. It was a sudden, snap decision, leading to a whirlwind of activity.

It was around Christmas when I decided I wanted to apply to law school. I called for an application to the law school in my area, the University at Buffalo School of Law. It would be my only possible choice given my new status as mother and homeowner. If I remember correctly, the information packet stated the deadline for applications was in April, and that I needed to include LSAT results. I remember getting online and searching for LSAT test information, hoping that I had not missed the examination. The good news was that I had not missed the February test date; the bad news was that I now had less than months to study for an exam I knew nothing about.

Not to be defeated, I jumped in the car and went to our local bookstore. In the reference section, I found four different LSAT preparation books. These books were LSAT practice guides which contained mock LSATs, including model test questions, hints on LSAT strategy, and practice tests.

I bought the books and for the next two months I did practice questions throughout my lunch hours at work. Every evening, I would spend about an hour or two working through the questions after putting the children to bed.

After becoming familiar with the format of the questions, I realized I was glad I had taken Logic in college. I realized that a logic course is very helpful in answering many of the LSAT questions. Becoming

Case Study: Kathy Daly, Esq

familiar with these types of questions provided me a level of comfort as the LSAT Test Day approached. I knew where my strengths and weaknesses were, and was able to manage my time appropriately to work on the areas that needed my concentration. This also provided a strategy for me to use during the actual LSAT.

That strategy was to move through each question quickly so that I did not run out of time. If a question was easily answered, I quickly filled in the answer bubble. If it was more difficult, I would see what type of question it was. If it was a type of question that I had success with in practice sessions, I would give the question a second look. If the question type fell in my weak category, I would mark the spot on the answer sheet and move on. I cannot stress how important it is to mark any skipped questions on your ANSWER sheet. This will prevent you from marking the next answer in that spot by mistake and possibly finding yourself at the end of the examination tragically wondering why there is an "extra" answer spot. At that point, you can only hope to find your error and be able to erase and re-mark your entire sheet within the time limit.

If you reach the end of the examination and have time left, then return to the questions which you skipped and try to answer them. Make an educated guess. If you can narrow it down to two choices, you have a 50/50 chance of adding another point to your score. That chance is better than knowing you will get no credit by not attempting to answer the question.

The last section of the LSAT is the Writing Sample. After reading the question, it is helpful to take a few minutes to compose your thoughts, and jot down a quick outline on scrap paper. The outline should just be a list of the points you wish to hit in your writing piece. This will help keep you on track as you are writing. This section is also timed, and

Case Study: Kathy Daly, Esq

the outline will keep you from losing your train of thought, and precious minutes. Keep your writing simple and organized. Law schools stress organized and logical arguments rather than flowery prose. Stick with your outline; do not get lost on tangents; keep it simple!

Lastly, but MOST importantly, make sure you get a good night's sleep before the LSAT Test Day. If possible, for the two or three nights prior to the exam go to bed at a reasonable hour and avoid any caffeine or alcohol consumption. Eat a healthy breakfast in the morning, but do not eat too many carbohydrates. A huge sweet roll may be great for Sunday mornings, but it will make your blood sugar and attention span crash about one hour into the exam. Take water into the exam with you.

Becoming dehydrated is very easy, and will cause fatigue, confusion, and difficulty concentrating. Also bring a snack to the exam with you. Chewy Granola bars, trail mixes, and protein bars are popular choices. Keeping your blood sugar up, but not too high, will allow your brain to function at its best.

My LSAT story had a happy ending. With concentrated preparation, I managed to achieve a score which fell well within the range of my selected law school's accepted candidates. My application was completed and submitted to University of Buffalo Law School two days before the deadline for a fall admission. Later that summer, I received a letter from UB…a FAT letter.

With all the distractions and challenges life presented, I was successful because I knew what I needed to achieve for UB and I approached the LSAT with a committed strategy and a preparation plan. I fit the preparation time I had available into my schedule and made it work. I approached the LSAT on Test Day with a high level of comfort from

Case Study: Kathy Daly, Esq

the hundreds of practice questions I had done in advance. This gave me the confidence I needed to calmly and efficiently use the time allotted and complete all the questions.

Conclusion

There is no easy cookie cutter guarantee to a high LSAT score. There is no "one" high LSAT score. What is your highest score depends on your choice of law school.

The way to achieve your highest possible score on the LSAT is through preparation, persistence, and planning. There are many excellent LSAT practice books, courses, and personal tutors available on the market to help you analyze your LSAT skills, and practice all of the sections of the LSAT; several have been highlighted and sampled in this book. Some resources are better geared for explaining the Games while others are better for Logical Reasoning. None can replace the value of using LSAC's past LSAT tests given in the field.

There is no shortcut for personalizing your preparation to your own learning style, and your own schedule and situation. As you read through the recommendations and the Case Studies in this book, you saw that to be the recurring theme. You have also seen that a holistic approach is going to give you an edge in a highly competitive field. The LSAT is not for the faint of heart, regardless where you intend to apply, how good you are at taking tests, or what optimal score you need to achieve.

By Test Day, you will have chosen your team of resources, mapped your plan of attack, and followed it wisely and thoroughly. You will have prepared as much as you can; you will be ready. Pack your plastic bag, arrive on time, and ace the LSAT.

It is just the beginning of a challenging, worthy, and fascinating profession. If you embrace the study of law it will change you forever.

Bibliography

Alpha-Score, "LSAT Scores Explained," Conversion Chart, **www. alpha-score.com/LSAT_Score_Conversion_Chart.html#chart**, September 11, 2008

Ball, Timothy, "Global Warming, The Cold, Hard Facts?" *Canada Free Press*, February 5, 2007, at **http://www.canadafreepress. com/2007/global-warming020507.htm**, March 2, 2008.

Barnes, Denise, "Teaching to the test," *The Washington Times*, August 13, 2001.

Blackwell Publishing Ltd., "Qigong Helped People Cope With Anxiety And Discrimination During SARS Outbreak." *Science Daily*, April 24, 2007, **http://www.sciencedaily.com/ releases/2007/04/070423091651.htm**, January 24, 2008.

Bowers v. Hardwick, 478 U.S. 186 (1986), (U.S. Supreme Court Opinion, and Briefs of Appellant and Appellee, Public Records).

Colcombe, Stanley J., Arthur F. Kramer, Kirk I. Erickson, Paige Scalf, Edward McAuley, Neal J. Cohen, Andrew Webb, Gerry J. Jerome, David X. Marquez, and Steriani Elavsky, "Cardiovascular fitness, cortical plasticity, and aging," *Proc Natl Acad Sci U S A*, 101(9):3316-3321, March 2, 2004, **http://www.pubmedcentral. nih.gov/articlerender.fcgi?artid=373255**, March 1, 2008.

Cpetrako, on "You Tube", **http://www.youtube.com/ watch?v=Bz1wHAVYi8Y**, You Tube, Inc., October 20, 2007.

Critical Thinking Foundation, "A Model for the National Assessment of Higher Order Thinking, Dillon Beach, CA, 2007, **http://www.criticalthinking.org/assessment/a-model-nal-assessment-hot.cfm**, February 11, 2008.

Cutts, Jay A., "Choosing an LSAT Prep Option: the Good, the Bad and The Real Ugly," Cutts Graduate Reviews, **http://www. cuttsreviews.com/jcutts/lsat/prepoptions.html**, February 10, 2008.

_____, Interview, November 30, 2007.

Daly, Kathy, Attorney, Rupp, Baase, Pfalzgraf, Cunningham & Coppola LLC, 1600 Liberty Building, Buffalo, NY 14202, Interview, February 26,, 2008.

Darwin, Charles, *The Origin of the Species by Means of Natural Selection*, **http://charles-darwin.classic-literature.co.uk/the-origin-of-species-by-means-of-natural-selection/ebook-page-25. asp** (Excerpt from Free Public Domain Books), February 25, 2008.

Facione, Peter A., "Critical Thinking: What It Is and Why It Counts," Insight Assessment, 2007 Update, California Academic Press, at **http://www.insightassessment.com/pdf_files/what&why2006. pdf**, March 1, 2008.

Felder, Richard and Barbara Solomon, **http://www.engr.ncsu. edu/learningstyles/ilsweb.html,** December 11, 2007.

Garrett, Elizabeth, *The Green Bag, Inc.*, 1998, reprinted at **www. law.uchicago.edu/socrates/soc_article.html**, December 11, 2007.

Gresser, Julian, *Piloting Through Chaos: Wise Leadership, Effective Negotiation for the 21st Century*, Five Rings Press, 1996.

Grout, Martha M., "Medical Acupuncture in the Treatment of Chronic Stress-Related Illness," *Acupuncture Today*, August 03:08, 2002, at **http://www.acupuncturetoday.com/archives2002/ aug/08grout.html**, March 1, 2008.

Hammer, Emanuel Frederick, "Post-hypnotic suggestion and test performance," *Journal of Clinical and Experimental Hypnosis*, 2, 1954, 178-185.

Husty, Dr. Todd, "Studies Prove Healing Power of Prayer," WESH COM, Orlando, FL, 2005, at **http://www.wesh.com/ health/3559756/detail.html**, February 10, 2008.

Internet Legal Research Group, **http://www.ilrg.com**, February 5, 2008.

Joas, Keri, "Lack of sleep limits academic attention span," Ripon College College Days, College Publisher, Inc., March 10, 2004, at **http://media.www.riponcollegedays.com/media/storage/ paper944/news/2004/03/10/Features/Lack-Of.Sleep**.Limits. Academic.Attention.Span-2416861.shtml, February 9, 2008.

Kaplan Publishing, *Kaplan LSAT 180*, Simon & Schuster, NY, 2001.

_____, *Kaplan MAT*, 2007-2008 Edition: Millers Analogies Test, Simon & Schuster, NY, 2007.

Killoran, David, *The PowerScore LSAT Logic Games Bible*, PowerScore Publishing, Hilton Head Island, SC, 2005.

Kolby, Jeff, *Master the LSAT*, Nova Press, Los Angeles, CA, 2007, 11, 17.

Law School Admission Council, Inc., *The Official LSAT Superprep*, LSAC, Newtown, PA, 2004, 3, 15, 40.

_____, **http://www.lsac.org**, February 10, 2008.

_____, LSAC Form 8LSN75, June 2007, sample tests online at **http://www.lsac.org/pdfs/test.pdf**, December 10, 2007.

Lawrence v. Texas, 539 U.S. 558 (2003), (U.S. Supreme Court Opinion, Briefs of Appellant and Appellee, Public Records).

Levine, Ann K., **http://lawschoolexpert.blogspot.com**, 1-877-LAW-SKOL, Interview, January 22, 2008.

Lighthouse Review, *The Ultimate Verbal and Vocabulary Builder for the SAT, ACT, GRE, GMAT, and LSAT*, The Lighthouse Review, Inc., Austin, TX, 2001.

Lincoln, Abraham, "Speech of Hon. Abraham Lincoln in Chicago, in reply to Senator Douglas," *Fort Wayne Weekly Republican*, July 21, 1858 (reporting text of Lincoln's speech on July 10, 1858, given in Chicago as part of the Lincoln-Douglas Debates).

Linehan, Kevin, "Improve Your Grades and Test Scores Through Hypnosis," **http://ontrachypnosis.com/better-study-exams.asp**, January 24, 2008.

Logan, Alan C., *The Brain Diet: The Connection Between Nutrition, Mental Health and Intelligence*, rev. ed., Nashville, TN, Cumberland House Publishing, Nashville, TN, 2007.

McGill University, **http://www.mcgill.ca/law-admissions/ undergraduates/admissions/**, February 1, 2008.

McKeown, Margaret G. and Mary E. Curtis, ed., *The Nature of Vocabulary Acquisition*, Lawrence Erlbaum Associates, Hillsdale, NJ, 1987, at **www.questia.com**, February 9, 2008.

Means, Kelly, Attorney, Wickens, Herzer, Panza, Cook & Batista, Co., 35765 Chester Road, Avon, OH 44011, (440) 930-8000, kmeans@wickenslaw.com, Interview, February 19, 2008.

Messina, PhD., James J. and Constance M. Messina, PhD., www. coping.org, September 11, 2008.

Mulcahy, Elaine, "Building the Mental Muscle," Australian Broadcasting Corporation, May 13, 2004, at **http://www.abc.net. au/science/features/mentalmuscle/**, March 1, 2008.

Naholowa'a, Makalika, Law Student, Columbia University School of Law, New York City, NY, Interview, December 27, 2007.

Philpotts, Eden, *Lying Prophets*, at **http://infomotions.com/etexts/ gutenberg/dirs/etext05/7lpro10.htm** (Public domain, excerpt adapted for Reading Comprehension example in this book).

Pinello, Daniel R., "Advice For Getting Into Law School," The

City University of New York, **http://www.danpinello.com/ LawSch.htm**, December 16, 2007.

Planned Parenthood v. Casey, 505 U.S. 833 (1992) (U.S. Supreme Court Opinion and Briefs of Appellant and Respondent, Public Records).

Plous, Scott, "Tips on Taking Multiple Choice Tests," **http://www. socialpsychology.org/testtips.htm#preparing**, January 5, 2008.

Qigong Research and Practice Center, www.qigonghealing.com, March 1, 2008.

Rawlinson, A.E.J., *Religious Reality*, 1918, at **http://www. authorama.com/religious-reality-3.html**, March 1, 2008. (Public domain excerpt adapted for Reading Comprehension example in this book).

Report of the President's Commission on the Accident at Three Mile Island, a public record posted at **http://www.pddoc.com/ tmi2/kemeny/**, March 1, 2008 (excerpt from Preface of Report condensed and adapted for Reading Comprehension example in this book).

Report of the President's Commission on the Assassination of President Kennedy, a public record at **http://www.archives. gov/research/jfk/warren-commission-report/chapter-1.html**, March 1, 2008 (excerpt from Chapter I, condensed and adapted in Reading Comprehension example in this book).

Robinson, Adam and Kevin Blevin, updated by Mindy Lee Myers, Bob Spruill, and Andrew Brody, *The Princeton Review - Cracking the LSAT*, Random House, NY, 2008.

Roe. v. Wade, 410 U.S. 113 (1972) (U.S. Supreme Court Opinion, Public Record).

Schnauzer, Mary, "Qigong: The Art of Self-Healing," *Perspectives in Psychiatric Care*, 42:53+, 2006, **www.questia.com**, February 10, 2008.

Sevilla, Charles M. and Lee Lorenz, *Disorder in the Court: Great Fractured Moments in Courtroom History*, W.W. Norton & Company, Inc., NY, 1999, Excerpt quoted from **www.cruiserjim. com/AmericanCourts.htm**, March 1, 2008.

Sims, Ariane, Blueprint LSAT Advice: *Mastering the LSAT: From Law School Admission to Law School Success*, Blueprint Test Preparation, **http://www.vault.com**, January 27, 2008.

Socrates, **http://www.philosophypages.com/ph/socr.htm**, 2007, January 28, 2008.

Stanton, Harry E. "Using Hypnosis to Overcome Examination Anxiety," *American Journal of Clinical Hypnosis,*" 35(3), 1993, 198-204.

Sternberg, Robert J. and Elena L. Grigorenko, "A Capsule History of Theory and Research on Style," in *Perspectives on Thinking, Learning, and Cognitive Styles*, Robert J. Sternberg and Li-fang Zhang, ed., Lawrence Ehrlbaum Associates, Mahwah, NJ, 2001, pp. 1-22, **www.questia.com**, January 12, 2008.

The Consus Group, **www.consusgroup.com/news/rankings/ law_schools/law_schools.asp**, January 31, 2008.

Top-Law-Schools.com, American law school rankings, http:// www.top-law-schools.com/rankings.html, and Canadian law school rankings, **http://www.top-law-schools.com/canadian-law-school-rankings.html**, February 1, 2008.

Torf, Bruce and Robert J Sternberg, *Understanding and Teaching the Intuitive Mind: Student and Teacher Learning*, Lawrence Ehrlbaum Associates, Mahwah, NJ, 2001, **http://www.questia.com**, 2008.

University of Chicago School of Law, **www.law.uchicago.edu/socrates/soc_article.html**, December 10, 2007.

University of Toronto Law School, **http://www.law.utoronto.ca/prosp_stdn_content.asp?itemPath=3/6/15/1/0&contentId=347**, February 1, 2008.

U.S. Dept. of Labor, Private Letter Ruling FMLA2005-1-A, August 26, 2005, at **http://www.dol.gov/esa/whd/opinion/FMLA/2005/2005_08_26_1A_FMLA.pdf**, March 1, 2008 (Public record excerpt adapted for Reading Comprehension example in this book).

U.S. News & World Report, Inc., **http://grad-schools.usnews.rankingsandreviews.com/usnews/edu/grad/rankings/law/brief/lawrank_brief.php**, January 31, 2008.

Virtue, Jeannine, "Boost Your Brain Power With Powerful 'Smart Foods'," March 26, 2007, **http://www.selfgrowth.com**, January 28, 2008.

Ward, Thomas B., Finke, Ronald A., Smith, Steven M., *Creativity and the Mind: Discover the Genius Within*, Plenum Press, NY, 1999.

Weinreb, Lloyd L., *Legal Reasoning The Use of Analogy in Legal Argument*, Cambridge University Press, Cambridge, MA, 2005.

White, Jeremy and David Pomerantz, "Law schools change LSAT policy," *The Tufts Daily*, December 1, 2006, **http://www.tuftsdaily.com**, January 30, 2008.

Wilkos, Mike, Virtual LSAT Proctor, **www.lsatproctor.com**, support@lsatproctor.com, Interview, October 28, 2007.

Yale University Law School, **http://www.law.yale.edu/admissions/howweevaluateapplications.htm**, and **http://www.law.yale.edu/admissions/profile.htm**, January 31, 2008.

Zi, Nancy, *The Art of Breathing: 6 Simple Lessons to Improve Performance, Health and Well-Being*, Rev. 4th ed., Frog, Ltd., Berkeley, CA, 2000.

Author Biography

Linda C. Ashar

A lawyer and educator for more than 20 years, Linda C. Ashar is a senior shareholder and chair of the labor and employment relations division of the law firm of Wickens, Herzer, Panza, Cook & Batista, Co. of Avon, Ohio. Her experience includes labor negotiations, arbitrations, litigation, counseling employers in a broad range of corporate and employment issues, and providing management training. She also is a freelance writer, painter, and breeder of Morgan horses and rare Irish Kerry Bog Ponies. She lives in Vermilion, Ohio with her husband Michael, who is also an attorney. When not at home in Ohio you are likely to find her at home on the shore of the Irish Sea in North Ireland.

Index

O

Opinion 38, 46, 50, 51, 64, 68,
        70, 139, 140, 141, 143,
        156, 178, 184, 186, 191,
        195, 198, 209, 211, 223

P

Passage 139, 140, 144, 149,
        155-158, 160, 162, 164,
        176-180, 182-184, 186,
        191, 203, 208
Practice 82, 86, 89, 91, 92, 94,
        98, 101-103, 106-108, 110,
        112, 115-122, 135, 136,
        142, 143, 153-155, 165,
        173, 176, 184-186, 191
Prepare 23, 24, 42, 72, 73, 78,
        82, 116, 163, 185, 187,
        239
Princeton Review 14, 70
Problem 132, 144, 168, 171,
        173, 175, 192, 193, 204,
        205, 208, 223

Q

Questions 76-79, 82, 85-87,
        89, 91, 92, 102, 121,
        135, 136, 138, 139, 144,

149, 153-157, 164, 165,
172, 173, 175, 176, 178,
183-186

R

Reading 43, 44, 62-65, 136,
        139, 143, 144, 175, 176,
        179, 184, 185
Reasoning 26-28, 37, 39-41,
        51, 54, 71, 76, 79, 124,
        125, 131, 136, 153-155,
        157, 159, 161, 162, 164,
        165, 172, 173, 184
Registration 239, 242
Resource 78, 79, 111, 117
Rules 37, 54, 56-62

S

Schedule 81, 105, 115-122
Score 13-17, 19-23, 25, 26,
        41-43, 71, 72
Section 43, 44, 46, 54, 59, 60,
        62-64, 70
Skills 77, 79, 135
Stress 102, 103, 106, 110, 111,
        113, 118
Study 23, 39, 40, 42, 54,
        63, 83, 90, 91, 96, 98,
        102, 103, 107, 111, 115,

How to Get Into the Top Graduate Schools: What You Need to Know About Getting Into Law, Medical, and Other Ivy League Schools Explained Simply

Now that you've passed your LSAT, your dream of getting into Harvard Law isn't far away. Learn exactly how to get into the top law schools around the country.

This comprehensive book details what the top schools are and how to apply. The book covers the admission process and gives you hints and tricks on what you need to get accepted into these prestigious schools. By following the suggestions in this book, you don't always need a 4.0 GPA or the highest score on your LSAT to be admitted into ivy league universities.

How to Get Into the Top Graduate Schools gives examples from students, professors, and admissions counselors. Learn from the pros so you can be sure to avoid costly mistakes and know exactly what is expected of your application.

ISBN-13: 978-1-60138-215-3
288 Pages • $24.95

To order call 1-800-814-1132 or visit www.atlantic-pub.com

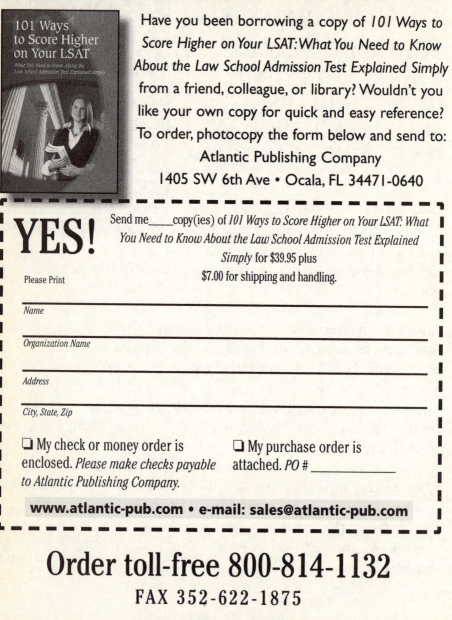